COMFORT
FOOD

DELECTABLE DEVOTIONS TO SATISFY THE SOUL

RAY COMFORT

Bridge-Logos
Alachua, Florida 32615

Bridge-Logos
Alachua, FL 32615 USA

Comfort Food
by Ray Comfort

Printed in the United States of America.

Library of Congress Catalog Card Number: 2008937332
International Standard Book Number 978-0-88270-528-6

Scripture quotations in this book are from *The Evidence Bible*, copyright 2003 by Bridge-Logos, Alachua, FL 32615. Used by permission.

G218.316.N.m809.35240

THE CHALLENGE

I noticed that a polite and seemingly sincere atheist has kindly challenged me, or any other Christian, to live the life of an unbeliever for just one month. In return, he would live the life of a Christian. The rule is that each person has to be open-minded to the possibility that they may be wrong in their beliefs. The Christian is not to read the Bible and he's not to go to church. The atheist will in turn read the Bible and go to church.

While I appreciate the kind gesture, it really illustrates that we Christians have a communication problem with some people. It's completely our fault. We haven't made the issue clear. So I'm going to try and make it very understandable. I will repeat and deliberately emphasize it, so that it hits the target. In doing this I risk sounding sarcastic. If that's how it comes across, I apologize.

Here we go: Christians are people who know the Lord. Let me repeat that. Christians are people who know the Lord. They know the Lord. Actually know Him. Experientially.

They know a Person, not a lifestyle. I'm talking about the God of the universe. They know Him.

I will now personalize this, but I am speaking on behalf of everyone who knows the Lord. I don't *believe* that He exists. I know Him. Personally. I have a living relationship with the Creator. I talk to Him through prayer, and He guides me through His Word and by His Holy Spirit. I have known the Lord since April 25, 1972, at 1:30 in the morning.

Perhaps I'm not making myself clear, so I will use an analogy. It's like actually *knowing* someone. Personally. It's like having a friendship with Him; a twenty-four-hour–a-day, 365-days-a-year intimate relationship. Therefore, it is evident that I can't live for a month being open to not knowing Him. All the "mistakes" in the Bible can't change that fact. All the hypocrisy committed by religious people in the past can't change it. All the atheists on God's Earth saying that He doesn't exist don't change it in the slightest. Darwin's theory can't change it. The storms of this life can't change it. If I get cancer and die a horrible death, it doesn't change the fact that I know the Lord. I not only know Him, but I love Him. I love Him with all of my heart, mind, soul, and strength. He is my life, He's my joy, my Creator, my Savior, my Lord, and my God.

And if I die for the cause of the gospel, my hope would be that the spilling of my blood would be a small testimony to those who don't know Him. My earnest hope and prayer would be that they would soften their sinful hearts, and repent and trust Jesus Christ, so that they too can testify to the unchanging truth that "… this is life eternal, that they might know you the only true God, and Jesus Christ, whom you have sent" (John 17:3).

"For I know whom I have believed, and am persuaded that he is able to keep that which I have committed to him against that day" (2 Timothy 1:12).

Making Up

Because of the fact that the natural man does not receive the things of the Spirit of God, we should relate to him in the natural realm, as Jesus did with the woman at the well. One way to do this is to compare spiritual truths to the things of this life. For instance, the place of contrition in one's life.

How can an unregenerate man understand such a deeply spiritual word as "contrition"? The answer is to relate it to something he can understand, such as a relationship with a woman he loves. When a man and a woman have an argument, they will experience a barrier between them. They will no longer feel close. That barrier is something called contention, and with contention comes a barrier of pride. Pride is a high wall that stops a man from seeing the one he loves. All he can see is his point of view, his rights, and his feelings. What is the door he can go through that will bring them close again? It is the lowly door of humility (one aspect of contrition).

The same principles apply to God, with whom the sinner is in contention. There is an enmity between the two (see Romans 8:7), and in this case, God is in the right and we are in the wrong. The Law of God lifts us up over that high wall so that we can see God's point of view. It gives us a glimpse into His righteousness and into our sinful and proud hearts. It humbles us so that we can find that place of contrition, or sorrow, and thus reconciliation through the blood of the Cross.

> "And almost all things are by the law purged with blood; and without shedding of blood is no remission" (Hebrews 9:22).

Crazy Door

I sat on my bike in our driveway watching our garage door open and shut as though a child had hold of the remote control. I went back and looked at the sensors at the bottom of the doors. There was nothing blocking them. Then I realized what had happened. The remote control button was stuck down, and it was sending the wrong signal.

There are people who are like my garage door. They don't know whether they are open or closed to the things of God. One moment they believe; then they don't. One moment they have peace; then they don't. What's their problem? Their remote button is jammed down on what the Bible calls unbelief. Nowadays we would call it mistrust. If we don't have faith in God, we mistrust Him. Try establishing a relationship with anyone you don't trust. Try it with your mom, dad, wife, boyfriend, girlfriend, or business partner. You won't get anywhere. So why should anyone think that they could have a relationship with God when they don't trust Him? Have faith in God. It's easy. He is faithful. If you don't trust Him, it means you think He's not trustworthy. You think He is devious, that He's a liar.

So what should you do to start an open relationship with God? The same thing you would do if you mistrusted a loved one. Start with an apology for insulting them with your lack of faith. Ask God to forgive you for such a terrible thing. And when you ask Him to forgive you for all your sins, make sure you "… ask in faith, nothing wavering. For he that wavers is like a wave of the sea driven with the wind and tossed. For let

4

not that man think that he shall receive anything of the Lord"
(James 1:6-7).

> *"Trust in the Lord with all your heart; and lean
> not unto your own understanding. In all your ways
> acknowledge him, and he shall direct your paths"*
> (Proverbs 3:5-6).

IT'S A DUH WORLD

Advertisers are now paying as much as two million dollars for a thirty-second advertisement during the Super Bowl. Experts tell us that they get a good financial return on their millions because human beings are tremendously influenced by what they see and hear. Apparently, if a celebrity is seen buying or doing something, many people will actually imitate what they see or hear. It seems that the biblical analogy of us being like sheep is applicable to this scenario.

"Thank you for joining us. Here is this evening's news: "Hollywood awarded its annual big honors last night for its best entertainment. Movies and television shows containing themes of violence, rape, and murder have been extremely popular throughout the whole year.

"In other news: After a comprehensive study, experts are mystified as to why there is a rising tide of violence, rape, and murder this year. Some have suggested that violence, rape, and murder are tied in with diet or perhaps with global warming.

"Thanks for joining us tonight for this news break. Let's return now to the second part of the exciting, award-winning movie, 'How to Rape and Murder and Get Away With It.' Then stay with us for 'Murder With a Chain Saw,' and 'How to Rape Your Neighbor.'"

"And be not conformed to this world: but be transformed by the renewing of your mind, that you may prove what is that good, and acceptable, and perfect, will of God" (Romans 12:2).

A Question About Marijuana

Someone asked, "While smoking tobacco is really, really awful, is smoking *cannabis* awful, too? It has medical uses, and as far as I can see, the conclusions regarding its side effects tend to be from cherry-picked data. It appears to me that the worst thing that could happen is that a dodgy dealer would sell it with some tobacco."

If marijuana is proven to have medical benefits, then it should be reproduced in pill form and made available through legitimate markets. Nothing should ever be taken into the lungs in smoke form. This has been proven to be detrimental to the health of any person. To legalize cannabis in its present form, in light of what has happened with alcohol, would be foolish.

The problem isn't with alcohol, it's with the crazy people that drive under its influence and kill people. If we think we have carnage on the roads now, wait until some foolhardy politicians legalize cannabis. It's called "dope" for a reason.

"Wherefore lay apart all filthiness and superfluity of naughtiness, and receive with meekness the engrafted word, which is able to save your souls" (James 1:21).

Warm Winds

I shudder when I read that John Wesley said that we should embrace every adversity. I shudder because I know how hard that can be for those of us who lack a solid faith in God. If we truly trust Him, we will know (as the Apostle Paul knew) "… that all things work together for good to them that love God, to them who are the called according to his purpose" (Romans 8:28).

I was ministering in Hawaii in the mid 1980's when I met up with a well-known preacher who I greatly respected. He was familiar with what I was teaching, and during a time of fellowship he gently told me that he didn't think that the Law of God should be used as a schoolmaster to bring sinners to Christ. I was shaken by his words. I knew that if we failed to evangelize biblically, we would fill the Church with false converts, but I couldn't seem to convince him of that fact. So I determined to write a book about what happens when the Law isn't used to bring the knowledge of sin. Over time, the publication became a best seller (*The Way of the Master)*, then an award-winning television program, and now it has become a popular radio program. And it was all sparked by that one man's negative words.

So even though someone's windy words may shake your tree, never let them uproot you, even if they come from a loving Christian brother. Instead, let them send the roots of your resolve down deep into the Word of God. Then make it your aim to do the will of God, and He will bless you and open doors for you to do His will, in His perfect timing.

> *"And he shall be like a tree planted by the rivers of water, that brings forth his fruit in his season; his leaf also shall not wither, and whatsoever he does shall prosper"* (Psalms 1:3).

THE ATHEIST'S BATTLE

John Lennon wrote, "Imagine there's no Heaven (it's easy if you try), with no hell below us, and above us only sky." Imagine that—death is the end, with no hope of eternal life. If that's the case, we will know nothing about it, because there won't be an afterlife. There will just be death. The Christian misses out on eternity.

But think of the poor atheist—if he doubts what he believes and begins to imagine that there is a God (it's easy if you try), with a hell below us, and above us more than sky. What if he imagines that there is actually a burning fire in the heart of the Earth (as science tells us), and that there is an infinite space above us (as science tells us)? Imagine that. Fire below. The infinite heavens above.

Like many nowadays, John Lennon imagined only sky. His mind was limited. However, the Christian's mind is not closed. By the grace of God, the Christian has expanded his horizon. Therefore, nothing is impossible for him.

"If you can believe, all things are possible to him that believes" (Mark 9:23).

Under the Jacket

When a doctor in Jerusalem knelt down to begin emergency treatment on a man who was critically wounded from a homicide bombing and ripped open his jacket, he didn't find gushing blood. Instead, he found an explosive belt. The wounded man was a would-be suicide bomber who was knocked out by the force of another blast before he was able to detonate his own explosive belt. The physician, who had rushed to the scene along with nurses from a nearby medical clinic, ran away as the wounded bomber began waving his arms. An Israeli policeman then shot the bomber and killed him.

This is the experience of every Christian. Outwardly, we looked innocent, but when the Holy Spirit pulled back the garb of self-righteousness, we were found to be rebels against all that was good and just. So what did God do? He executed us on the spot. God reckoned me dead the moment I surrendered to the Savior. I was legally executed with Jesus Christ. The

Apostle Paul spoke of this amazing fact when he said, "I am crucified with Christ: nevertheless I live; yet not I, but Christ lives in me: and the life which I now live in the flesh I live by the faith of the Son of God, who loved me, and gave himself for me" (Galatians 2:20). It has been well said that if we are born once, we will die twice (the first and the second death), but if we are born twice, we will only die once. (See John 3 for further details.)

"Jesus answered and said to him, Verily, verily, I say to you, Except a man be born again, he cannot see the kingdom of God" (John 3:3).

CUTTING EDGE

CBS ran a human-interest story about a barber in Kalamazoo, Michigan, who, after thirty-eight years of cutting his customers' hair, went blind. However, his faithful customers continued to come to him, and he continued cutting by memory and by feel.

The story reminded my wife and me of a local dentist we wanted to support some years ago. We heard that he was on the cutting edge of dentistry, but, unbeknown to us, the poor man suffered from tremors in his hands. I was filled with sympathy for him during the procedure, but I will never go back. The experience was a nightmare. Sue will never forget seeing me come out with a white face and blood splatters around my mouth. Her experience was just as bad.

Some people have a similar experience with church. It's a nightmare of boredom and they never want to go back again. Or even worse, they like it because the preacher keeps them entertained. However, if he is not faithful to God's Word and does not preach against sin, the man is blind. And Jesus warned that when the blind lead the blind, both will fall into the ditch.

> *"Let them alone: they be blind leaders of the blind. And if the blind lead the blind, both shall fall into the ditch"* (Matthew 15:14).

A Question From an Atheist

"If Jesus is God and God is omniscient," the atheist asked, "what sense does it make for Him to have himself killed? I mean, if He wanted to forgive us, why not just forgive us? Why all the blood? Also, if Jesus was without sin, how is it moral for an innocent to receive punishment for another's crimes, in this case the 'sins' of humanity?"

Without an understanding of God's law, we can never understand the justice of God. It is when we realize that God's standard of goodness is absolute moral perfection, called holiness, that we can understand the meaning of what the Bible calls atonement. Think of a man who commits a terrible crime and runs from the law. He is no longer a "just" man. He is a fugitive from justice. He is in debt to the law he has violated. Civil law will track him like a hungry hound dog to the ends of the Earth.

Think of it—with all our faults and failures, we will spend millions of dollars to bring even one serious criminal to justice. That's because we are moral beings. So if we, with all our sins, care about justice, how much more will a perfect and holy God care? His holiness will make sure that every murderer, rapist, thief, and liar will come to justice. But because He is

omniscient and therefore sees even our thought life, He will also punish lust, which He considers adultery of the heart, and hatred, which He considers to be murder. Every transgression of His law must receive absolute justice, and who of us is without sin? Who of us hasn't lied, stolen, or looked with lust on another person? That means we are in big trouble with God. His wrath abides on us. We have a big problem. The Bible warns that if God were to give justice to every fugitive, we would all justly end up in a place called hell. Each of us has broken His law, and we are in debt to eternal justice.

So what can we offer God in payment for our sins? What will make things right? How can we make atonement? Should we try to live good lives? We can't. It's too late. We are already guilty criminals. Reformation of our lives can't make atonement for our sins. We would merely be reformed criminals. What then will appease God? Can we offer Him all the gold of the Earth to pay our fine? No. He already owns all the gold. We don't have anything of value to pay the fine and make atonement for our sins, let alone the sins of the world. Not even our blood could make atonement for our sins. We are in a hopeless position, waiting for death to arrest us and cast us into an eternal prison called hell.

Now here is the answer to the question, "Why all the blood?" The Bible says that this holy God is rich in mercy, and because of His great love, He provided atonement himself. He became a human being in the person of Jesus of Nazareth. Almighty God created a human body and filled that body like a hand fills a glove. Jesus Christ was called "the express image of the invisible God." (See Colossians 1:15.) And He did this amazing thing for the precise purpose of paying for the sins of the world. The most precious possession on the face of this

Earth is not gold, silver, oil, or diamonds. It is the precious blood of the Savior, and He gave His life's blood to pay the price. That's why He cried, "It is finished!" as he breathed His last breath on the cross. In other words, the debt had been paid. His precious blood made atonement. It satisfied eternal justice.

Then God raised Him from the dead, and now death has no legal dominion over those who repent and trust in Him. Their case is dismissed. They are proclaimed, "Not guilty." God commutes their death sentence because another paid their fine. But it is more than that. God imputes righteousness to us. In other words, we are not just forgiven criminals. Through the gospel, He makes us perfectly right with himself. We can now live. So if you are not right with God, put aside the issues that bother you for a moment—evolution, hypocrisy, "mistakes" in the Bible—and ask yourself this most sobering of questions: "What shall it profit a man, if he shall gain the whole world, and lose his own soul?" (Mark 8:36). Today, if you hear His voice, don't harden your heart.

"Whosoever will come after me, let him deny himself, and take up his cross, and follow me" (Mark 8:34).

Just Curious

"I'm just curious," asks one seeker, "am I correct in assuming that Ray and other Christians here all believe that Catholics, Methodists, Lutherans, Episcopalians, and various other sects of Christianity are all false Christians, *unless* they are born again, and become evangelical fundamentalists?"

The Bible doesn't mention "Catholics, Methodists, Lutherans, Episcopalians, and various other sects." The Scriptures simply have two categories—the just and the unjust. The *just* are those whom God has justified, made right with himself through faith in Jesus. The *unjust* are those who are still

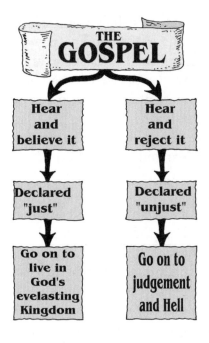

THE
GOSPEL

Hear and believe it → Declared "just" → Go on to live in God's evelasting Kingdom

Hear and reject it → Declared "unjust" → Go on to judgement and Hell

in their sins. The Bible warns that God will see to it that all wicked people get exactly what they have coming: "So shall it be at the end of the world: the angels shall come forth, and sever the wicked from among the just, and shall cast them into the furnace of fire: there shall be wailing and gnashing of teeth" (Matthew 13:49-50). That's good news for those who care about justice.

So the question is: How is a person *justified*? That is what Martin Luther, who was a Catholic monk, asked hundreds of years ago. He found, through reading the Bible, that we are freely justified by God's mercy. The criminal is guilty, but the Judge pays his fine. That's mercy. In Christ, God acquits us in the courtroom because Jesus paid our fine. Everlasting life is the gift of God. (See Romans 6:23.) No one has to be "religious" to try and earn salvation from death. So who are the true Christians? Here is that answer from the Bible: "Nevertheless the foundation of God stands sure, having this seal, The Lord knows them that are his. And, Let everyone that names the name of Christ depart from iniquity'" (2 Timothy 2:19). So make sure you are the Lord's, and that when you name the name of Christ, you depart from iniquity, the violation of God's law.

"That the righteousness of the law might be fulfilled in us, who walk not after the flesh, but after the Spirit" (Romans 8:4).

Big Dog Killed

A friend of mine told me that a Chihuahua killed his buddy's Great Dane. They got into a fight, and within two minutes the Chihuahua had killed the massive dog. Yep. The Great Dane choked on it.

Speaking of dogs, I have often heard skeptics say that we humans are the most intelligent of the species. When I hear someone say that, I ask if they can round up 3,000 sheep in twenty seconds, or catch a Frisbee in their mouths while running and jumping six feet into the air. Can they sniff out illicit drugs at an airport?

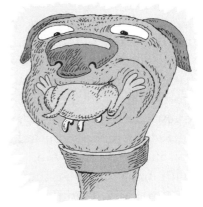

While I'm not sure if mankind is the most intelligent being in all of creation, Albert Einstein seems to have made up his mind on the issue. He said, "Only two things are infinite, the universe and human stupidity, and I'm not sure about the former." Evolution and atheism tend to make me side with Albert.

"What is man, that you are mindful of him? and the son of man, that you visit him?" (Psalm 8:4).

Who Cares?

"Lusting after women or property ... who cares?" asked my skeptical friend. "That 'thought' is a crime is absurd. If you don't act on it, why should you be punished? Even if you dwell on it."

The thought that merely thinking could be a crime does seem absurd. Absurd, that is, until you realize that if you are caught thinking about killing the President of the United States, you will find yourself in serious violation of civil law. You don't have to do the act. You simply have to be thinking about it.

So what would our skeptical questioner say to that? Let me try and predict his words. He would probably say something like, "That's different. Conspiracy to murder the president is a serious crime." And that's the point. He doesn't think that pornography in the mind is a serious crime. God does. Our questioner's moral standards are extremely low. God's are incredibly high. If you and I have a seething hatred in our heart for another person, God sees that as murder. And if we burn with unlawful sexual thoughts towards another human being, God sees that as adultery.

So to answer our skeptic's question: "Lusting after women or property … who cares?" God cares. He cares about justice big time, and He will see to it that the guilty will get their just deserts. Adulterers and murderers will end up damned in a terrible place called hell. Who cares? I do, and I'm not the only one.

"Do you not know that the unrighteous shall not inherit the kingdom of God? Be not deceived: neither fornicators, nor idolaters, nor adulterers, nor effeminate, nor abusers of themselves with mankind, nor thieves, nor covetous, nor drunkards, nor revilers, nor extortioners, shall inherit the kingdom of God" (1 Corinthians 6:9-10).

WATCH OUT FOR SEX OFFENDERS

When a nineteen-year-old student was kidnapped in Nevada, police informed the other students that there were a total of ninety-three registered sex offenders living within a one-mile radius of the university. You can find out if there is one living in your area, someone who is watching your sister, child, your mother, or your wife. All you have to do is type your zip code into the U.S. Sexual Offender Database of the 374,270 sexual predators. They are the registered offenders. You can be sure, however, that most are not registered.

How do you become a "registered" sex offender? You simply have to break the law. Let's do a test to see if you are one. Jesus said whoever "… looks on a woman to lust after her has committed adultery already with her already in his heart" (Matthew 5:28). Have you ever done that? If you have, then you are guilty of breaking God's law and your name is registered in Heaven as a sex offender. However, upon your repentance and faith in Jesus, God wipes your slate clean because of what He did on the cross.

> *"For the wages of sin is death; but the gift of God is eternal life through Jesus Christ our Lord"* (Romans 6:23).

Fools Mock at Sin

Florida woman was tried for vehicular manslaughter after running down a man who was riding a bike. As she was awaiting the verdict (which was predicted to be a one-to-four-year sentence), she took a phone call from a friend and laughed as he made jokes about the victim's death. When the judge heard the recorded phone call, he threw the book at her, and gave her the maximum sentence of more than ten years. Why did he do that? Because her laughter revealed that she had no contrition, or true sorrow. She didn't see the seriousness of her crime.

What is it that will bring swift mercy from the Judge of the universe? What is it that will open the door of the grace of God to guilty sinners? It is what the Bible calls *godly sorrow*. It is only when we see the seriousness of our transgressions against God that we will have godly sorrow, and it is godly sorrow that "works repentance." Each of us has a choice. We can be a fool and mock at sin, or we can see sin as being *exceedingly sinful*. You have God's Word on it: He will throw the Book at the proud and impenitent heart, but He will give grace to the humble. So humble yourself today, acknowledge your sins, and as you trust in the Savior, you will taste the grace of God.

"For godly sorrow works repentance to salvation not to be repented of: but the sorrow of the world works death" (2 Corinthians 7:10).

FRANK MILLSTONE

I had just finished open-air preaching at Huntington Beach when a friend showed up with his eight-year-old daughter. She's a sweet little kid with a strong faith in God. Some time later I saw him conversing with an atheist named Frank. Frank had been heckling me, and seemed to consider himself to be quite an intellectual. When my friend's little girl told him that she believed in God, Frank bent down and in a fatherly way told her that God was just like Santa Claus—He didn't exist.  How could he do such a thing? I was horrified. He was like a poor, mentally challenged man sticking a fork into a live power outlet.

I said, "Frank, do you know what a millstone is?" He did. I said, "Do you remember what Jesus said about millstones?" He said he had never read the Bible. My heart went out to him. He didn't know what he had just done. Poor Frank. The Bible is the greatest selling book of all time, yet he had never read it. If you are tempted to follow in Frank's footsteps, here's what Jesus said: "And whosoever shall offend one of these little ones that believe in me, it is better for him that a millstone were hanged about his neck, and he were cast into the sea" (Mark 9:41-43).

> *"But Jesus said, Suffer little children, and forbid them not, to come to me: for of such is the kingdom of heaven"* (Matthew 19:14).

DUMB MUTT

It was some time in the early hours of the morning in July, 1995. We had bought a new home and the move had provided an opportunity to break our new puppy of the habit of sleeping in our bed. However, in the blackness of the night I could see the dumb dog lying on the pillow next to me. I had just awakened from a deep sleep, and a thousand thoughts raced through my dozy mind as to why this pup would be back in bed with us.

I reached out my hand and stroked the animal, but felt confused. Its fur seemed a little strange. As I extended my hand to touch it again, to my horror it began to levitate! In the eerie darkness, I could see the animal's entire body actually lifting itself up off the pillow and into the air.

I regained my composure, then apologized to my wife, Sue, for stroking her hair during the night, and went back to sleep, feeling rather stupid. (From my book, *101 of the Dumbest Things People Have Done,* published by Bridge-Logos in June, 2008.)

"I WOULD FREELY GIVE MY EYES IF YOU MIGHT BUT SEE CHRIST, AND I WOULD WILLINGLY GIVE MY HANDS IF YOU MIGHT BUT LAY HOLD ON HIM."
CHARLES SPURGEON,
THE PRINCE OF PREACHERS:

From
Spurgeon Gold

Interesting Thread

David W. Irish said, "I think that whether the Scriptures are true or not is irrelevant. Christianity is a mind-set, a philosophy, a way of living that depends on the practitioners/believers practicing it more than anything … When I was a Christian …"

David, it's important to speak truthfully about our experiences by using the correct terminology. Rather than saying, "When I was a Christian," you should say, "When I professed to be a Christian," or, to be biblically sound, "When I was a false convert." Your spurious experience isn't surprising, because you believe that being a Christian is "a mind-set, a philosophy, a way of living." I had those things in my surfing days. That is not the definition of what a Christian has. Rather, a Christian is someone who knows the Lord. (See John 17:3.)

A false convert doesn't know Him. (See 1 John 2:3-4 and 1 John 4:6-8.) He fakes it, but time exposes his hypocrisy. Judas is a good example of a false convert. He faked it for three and a half years. He was so trusted that he looked after the finances, but the Bible says he was a thief. (See John 12:6.) When Jesus said that one of the disciples would betray Him, each one said, "Is it I, Lord?" They suspected themselves, rather than the trusted treasurer. When Judas went out to betray Jesus, some of the disciples thought that he went to give money to the poor. He fooled everyone but

God. The Scriptures tell us that Jesus knew from the beginning who would betray Him. (See John 6:70.)

Judas had no idea who Jesus was, even though he ate and drank with Him, as does the false convert when taking communion. Judas didn't see Him as the ultimate treasure in an earthen vessel—God manifest in the flesh. When a woman broke an alabaster box of precious ointment and poured it on His feet, as an act of worship, Judas complained that the money should have been given to the poor instead. Jesus wasn't worth it. He was only worth about thirty pieces of silver.

David, if you respond to me by saying that you were a genuine Christian, then you are admitting that you knew the Lord, that Jesus rose from the dead, and therefore Christianity is true. If you didn't know the Lord, then you were a false convert. You were either one or the other.

Another thought is, if you are of the disposition that you could be deceived, how do you know that it's not happening again? The essence of deception is that the deceived person doesn't know when he or she is deceived. That is why we need God's Word as a guide.

If I had been through your experience, I would be as upset as you. Remember that Judas ended up hanging himself. So be careful when you dine with atheists, because the sweet dishes they serve up contain undetected poison that will find its way into your very heart. They will feed you tasty Bible verses out of context, misquotes, and half-truths. The devil will give you enough rope to hang yourself. I would hate for that to happen to you.

"Jesus said to him, I am the way, the truth, and the life: no man comes to the Father, but by me" (John 14:6).

Personal Politics

While I am concerned about the economy, securing our borders, providing full employment, and other timely issues, these fade into the background over one crucial issue. Does the candidate advocate the murder of babies in the womb? If he (or she) does, I will throw his eloquence and fiscal brilliance to the wind. He wouldn't get my vote if he were the last person on God's fair Earth. Yes, I know that if he were the last person on the Earth, I wouldn't be here to vote for him. But you know what I mean.

> *"The Lord has called me from the womb; from the bowels of my mother has he made mention of my name"* (Isaiah 49:1).

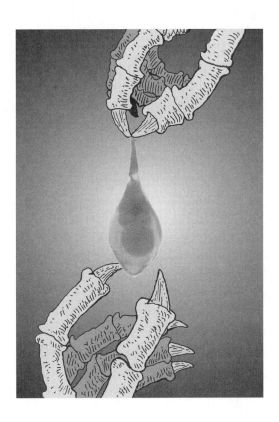

AMERICA'S GODLY HERITAGE

God-haters will hate to hear that the words "In God We Trust," which are found on our currency, have been part of America's heritage for more than 140 years. According to the U.S. Treasury, Secretary of the Treasury Salmon P. Chase received many appeals from devout persons throughout the country, urging that the United States recognize the Deity on United States coins. From Treasury Department records, it appears that the first such appeal came in a letter dated November 13, 1861:

"Dear Sir: One fact touching our currency has hitherto been seriously overlooked. I mean the recognition of the Almighty God in some form on our coins. . . . You are probably a Christian. What if our Republic were not shattered beyond reconstruction? Would not the antiquaries of succeeding centuries rightly reason from our past that we were a heathen nation?"

As a result, Secretary Chase instructed James Pollock, Director of the Mint of Philadelphia, to prepare a motto, in a letter dated November 20, 1861:

"Dear Sir: No nation can be strong except in the strength of God, or safe except in His defense. The trust of our people in God should be declared on our national coins."

IN GOD WE TRUST first appeared on the 1864 two-cent coin.

"Blessed are all they that put their trust in him"
(Psalm 2:12).

Delete Files

In Jacksonville, Florida, a woman employee saw an advertisement for what she thought was her job. She was convinced that she was going to be fired. So late one Sunday night, she crept into the Mandarin office where she worked at Steven E. Hutchins Architects and deleted seven years' worth of architectural drawings. The company put the value of the vaporized files at $2.5 million. The woman confessed to the crime and faced a five-year prison sentence. Here is the most interesting part of the story: the woman was not going to be fired. The owner of the business said that the job listing was for his wife's business—not his.

This story exemplifies the ungodly, who, in their rage against God, don't know that it is their own lives that they are deleting. Instead of keeping their most precious possession, they will lose it and reap the terrible reward of their error—eternal justice. And they will have no one to blame but themselves.

> *"He that believes on him is not condemned: but he that believes not is condemned already, because he has not believed in the name of the only begotten Son of God"* (John 3:18).

ARGUING ABOUT THE BIBLE

How do you respond to people when they say the Bible was written by a bunch of crazy people and you have to be crazy to believe it?

I would say, "Let's not argue about the inspiration of the Bible for a moment," and then I would take them through the Commandments. Jesus didn't say, "Go into all the world and convince people that the Bible is the Word of God." It is the *gospel* that is the power of God for salvation, and the way to give the arrow of the gospel its thrust is to put it into the bow of the Law.

We often hear that Christianity stands or falls on the validity of Scripture. I respectfully disagree. I believe the Bible is God's Word. There's no argument there. But my salvation isn't dependent upon that fact, because I wasn't converted by the Bible. I was converted by the power of God, and when I picked up a Bible, it simply explained what had happened to me.

In our sincere efforts to convince a sinful world, we tend to use intellectual arguments—I'm often guilty of this—when the ultimate proof is the power of God to transform the human heart. I didn't come to Christ through an intellectual argument, and my faith doesn't stand on human wisdom, so why should I try and bring others through that door?

If the whole scientific world came together and disproved the Bible, and archeologists found what were proved to be the bones of Jesus, it wouldn't shake my faith in the slightest. Not at all. This is what Paul speaks about in 1 Corinthians 2:4-5, when he says that the Christian's faith doesn't stand "in the wisdom of men, but in the power of God."

> "IT TAKES NO BRAINS TO BE AN ATHEIST.
> ANY STUPID PERSON CAN DENY THE EXISTENCE OF
> A SUPERNATURAL POWER BECAUSE MAN'S PHYSICAL
> SENSES CANNOT DETECT IT. BUT THERE CANNOT
> BE IGNORED THE INFLUENCE OF CONSCIENCE,
> THE RESPECT WE FEEL FOR THE MORAL LAW, THE
> MYSTERY OF FIRST LIFE ... OR THE MARVELOUS ORDER
> IN WHICH THE UNIVERSE MOVES ABOUT US ON THIS EARTH. ALL
> THESE EVIDENCE THE HANDIWORK OF THE BENEFICENT DEITY....
> THAT DEITY IS THE GOD OF THE BIBLE AND JESUS CHRIST,
> HIS SON"
> (DWIGHT EISENHOWER, FROM *The Evidence Bible*).

Remember, the Scriptures did not convert the early Christians. They were saved by a *spoken* message instead. Most couldn't read anyway. The New Testament hadn't been compiled. There was no such thing as the printing press.

If you believe that the foundation for our faith is the written Scriptures rather than in the person of Jesus Christ, I have some questions for you. When did Christianity begin? Was it on the Day of Pentecost when 3,000 people were converted by the power of God, or did it have to wait until the New Testament was compiled in 200 AD?

So don't feel that it's your mandate to convince anyone of the inspiration of the Word of God. You will never do it while they love their sins. For every reasonable argument you come up with, they will come back with a 101 atrocities and injustices in the Bible.

Instead, send the arrow of the gospel that is thrust by using the Law of God to bring the knowledge of sin. Make the sinner thirst after righteousness, without which, he will perish. Then, once he is born again and comes to know the Lord, the Scriptures will open up to him. Until that time, the things of God will seem foolishness to him, as the Scriptures declare.

"All scripture is given by inspiration of God, and is profitable for doctrine, for reproof, for correction, for

instruction in righteousness: that the man of God may be perfect, thoroughly furnished to all good works" (2 Timothy 3:16).

"The fool has said in his heart, There is no God. They are corrupt, they have done abominable works, there is none that does good" (Psalm 14:1).

Born That Way

"Ray," asks a seeker, "why, then, did God make people homosexual? Isn't this cruel? I suppose you will say that they choose to be homosexual. I think you and I know this is absurd. Why, then, would God make them this way only to prohibit the strongest of all urges in people?"

Good question. It's common for Christians to say that homosexuals weren't born "that way," that they instead choose that lifestyle. I think we are all born "that way" because we inherit a sinful nature. I didn't have to teach my children to lie, to steal, or to be selfish. They naturally knew how to do that. I had to teach them to do what was right. As each of us grows from childhood, we have the potential to be a fornicator, a liar, a thief, an adulterer, a pervert, a homosexual, a drunkard, a murderer, a rapist, or a pedophile. So we didn't choose the sinful nature, but we did choose to follow a particular sin.

The good news is that God does not only forgive sin, but that He gives us a new heart, a new inner self, that desires to do that which pleases Him—to do that which is right. Hopefully, if you are still in your sins, you will repent and trust the Savior before the Day of Judgment, when the door of mercy will close. After that happens, there won't be a hope in hell, so take sin seriously.

> "*Do you not know that the unrighteous shall not inherit the kingdom of God? Be not deceived: Neither fornicators, nor idolaters, nor adulterers, nor effeminate* [homosexuals], *nor abusers of themselves with mankind* [Sodomites], *nor thieves, nor covetous, nor drunkards, nor revilers, nor extortioners, shall inherit the kingdom of God. And such were some of you: but you are washed, but you are sanctified, but you are justified in the name of the Lord Jesus, and by the Spirit of our God*" (1 Corinthians 6:9-11).

How to Deal With Hell

If you are too intelligent to become an atheist, here's a good way to temporarily handle the "hell problem." Say to yourself that God is all loving and all forgiving, and that He would never create a place called hell. Then negate the need for retribution by calling homosexuality "gay," and adultery "an affair." Call lies "fibs," corporate theft "blue collar crime," gambling "gaming," and murder "temporary insanity." There's one more call. Make sure you call yourself "deceived."

Those who don't believe in hell are deceived into thinking that God is corrupt. Think for a moment as to why we have court systems. It's because we are moral beings. We are made in the image of God. That's what separates us from the beasts. We believe in justice and truth. When a man commits a murder, a good judge could never turn a blind eye to his crimes. If he did, then he's corrupt, and should be brought to justice himself. In the 1990's, statistics reveal that there were approximately 100,000 unsolved murders in the United States. The Bible warns that God will not turn a blind eye to the taking of those 100,000 precious human lives. Or think of actor George Clooney's experience in East Africa, where he met a young woman who had been viciously raped by Sudanese rebels. They then burned her, and cut off her lips so she couldn't talk. Those wicked men will be brought to absolute justice, and it will be thorough, utterly fearful, and irrevocably eternal.

But this same holy Creator warns that He considers hatred to be murder and lust to be adultery. He warns that lying lips are an abomination to Him, and all liars will be cast into the lake of fire. (See Revelation 21:8.) Who of us is without guilt in sinning against God? Each of us has a multitude of sins that will come to light on what the Bible calls the Day of Wrath, unless we have been forgiven through faith in the Savior

> *"But the fearful, and unbelieving, and the abominable, and murderers, and whoremongers, and sorcerers, and idolaters, and all liars, shall have their part in the lake which burns with fire and brimstone: which is the second death"* (Revelation 21:8).

How Smart Is Your Right Foot?

I always smile when people say that they are the masters of their own destiny. If we are in control of our destinies, surely we would be in control of our own bodies. Yet, the human body has a mind of its own. If you think that you are in control, then stop yourself from blinking. You can't. You are a slave to it, as well as a slave to sleeping, and daily bodily functions. Your liver, lungs, kidneys, heart, and other vital organs work independently of your will. You can't stop yourself from dreaming or thinking, because your subconscious has a mind of its own.

You can't even outsmart your right foot, because God has pre-programmed your brain to do certain things that are totally independent of your will. Don't believe it? Then try this. Sit down and lift your right foot off the floor and make clockwise circles. Now, while doing this, draw the number 6 in the air with your right hand. Your foot will change direction, if you are normal.

> *"O house of Israel, cannot I do with you as this potter? says the Lord. Behold, as the clay is in the potter's hand, so are you in my hand"* (Jeremiah 18:6).

THE GAY "CHRISTIAN"

People often ask how to respond to those who are homosexuals and yet consider themselves to be Christians. While a fornicator, a homosexual, an adulterer, a thief, and a liar can *become* Christians, it is important to understand that they cannot remain in their sins. If someone does, he is simply a pretender, a hypocrite. To be a Christian, you must stop your sinful lifestyle, which is commonly called *repentance*.

So how do you tell someone this without causing undue offense? I would witness to him using God's Law, the Ten

"MAN WILL BELIEVE ANYTHING, AS LONG AS IT'S NOT IN THE BIBLE."
NAPOLEON BONAPARTE

Commandments. I wouldn't mention the homosexual issue until he is humbled, and sin is seen in its true light. There's a very good reason for this. No proud person can see the nature of his own sins. He is blinded by pride. If you have counseled married couples, you will know this to be true. If there is no humility, there will not be an open ear to reason. So the Law should be used to humble the human heart, reveal sin in its true light, and, if possible, show the person his error, and his great danger.

"For this cause God gave them up to vile affections: for even their women did change the natural use into that which is against nature: and likewise also the men, leaving the natural use of the woman, burned in their lust one toward another; men with men working that which is unseemly, and receiving in themselves that recompense of their error which was meet" (Romans 1:26-27).

MEN IN WHITE COATS

Years ago, a man carrying a large ladder and wearing a white coat walked into a courtroom while it was in session. He leaned the ladder against the wall, climbed it, and took the court clock. He was a thief. I guess he took the time to do this in response to some sort of dare.

You may have noticed that doctors on infomercials who peddle medicinal products usually wear white coats. The white coat helps them get away with more than time. It supposedly shows us that they are trustworthy. However, many a man in a white coat has carried on some illegitimate operation until the law caught up with him. Despite this, most genuine doctors still wear white coats, because, arguably, it makes us feel more comfortable as they poke, prod, and pry.

Some preachers also wear white coats. It may impress some, but we should reserve our respect for the man who is clothed in humility. Is your pastor humble of heart? Or is he a wolf in sheep's clothing, of whom Jesus warned us to  beware? To find out, you should listen to what comes out of his mouth, because the mouth speaks from the abundance of the heart, and out of the heart come the issues of life. Does he preach the unadulterated gospel? Does he have a deep concern for the lost? Does he treat his wife with the utmost respect? Is he separated from the world? Is he clean in his humor? Does he love and preach from the Scriptures? Does he walk in the fear of God? If not, it would be wise to question if you should be sitting under his teaching and supporting his ministry.

"But you, O man of God, flee these things; and follow after righteousness, godliness, faith, love, patience, meekness" (1 Timothy 6:11).

THE BOUNDARIES

We were in Green Bay, Wisconsin, on a cold day in December, and had lost the key to our hotel room. To our surprise, the desk clerk gave us another one without asking to see our ID. She didn't even ask for our names. If we had done the same thing in California, they would have wanted our names, ID's, thumbprints, voice recognition, a deposit, and a thirty-five-dollar key fee.

There was a time in the United States when you didn't have to lock your car or the front door of your house. It was a time when you could trust your neighbors and they could trust you. There was a time when your wife could go shopping after dark and not fear being raped, or you could go camping and not end up being murdered. There were crimes, but it was nothing like what we see nowadays.

What has happened to our nation? We have become what the Bible calls lawless. We have forsaken God's Law, and when that happens, we forsake the fear of God. When a nation loses the fear of the Lord, it loses its moral boundaries. Thus, we have contemporary America.

Most Christians know that salvation for the United States won't come through economic policies, or through a change of government. It can only come through a change of heart, and only God can change a sin-loving heart into one that loves righteousness. However, it is important for us to remember that the agenda of the Church in the Book of Acts wasn't to make Israel the greatest political and economic nation on Earth. It was simply to preach the gospel and see sinners saved from the wrath of a holy God. It is easy for us to get caught up in the temporal when we should be putting our energies into the eternal.

> *"Blessed is the nation whose God is the Lord; and the people whom he has chosen for his own inheritance"* (Psalm 33:12).

THE POWER OF REASON

It is easy to prove the reality of the existence of hell to a reasoning person. However, this can't be done when a person denies that which is axiomatic. When a human being denies God's existence, he stands on his own oxygen hose. In his futile effort to break free from moral accountability, he cuts himself off from the very thing that can allow him to keep the precious life he so loves—his God-given power of reason. Charles Spurgeon called such a person, a "learned fool."

> *"Because that, when they knew God, they glorified him not as God, neither were thankful; but became vain in their imaginations, and their foolish heart was darkened"* (Romans 1:21).

THE BLIND FAITHFUL

Since falling away from my faith in evolution back in 1972, I can't help but notice the evolutionist's intolerance toward freedom of thought. We see this in staunch believers in evolution, who hold to their faith like a religion. They exalt Charles Darwin into papal infallibility. He is robed in pure white, as he stands high upon the balcony of time, waving his hand to the faithful. A word from his lips is the gospel truth, and his great commission to true believers is to embark on a crusade, and bring down the swift sword of intolerance upon all who do not embrace the true faith.

Yet Darwin was nothing but a racist, a bigot of a man, who held to the belief that black people are inferior to whites. He said: "At some future period not very distant as measured by centuries, the civilized races of man will almost certainly exterminate and replace the savage races throughout the world. At the same time the anthropomorphous apes . . . will no doubt be exterminated. The break between man and his nearest Allies will then be wider, for it will intervene between man in a more civilized state, as we may hope, even than the Caucasian, and some ape as low as the baboon, instead of as now between the Negro or Australian and the gorilla." (*The Descent of Man*, "The Races of Man" 1874, p. 178.)

The above is only one of many racist beliefs that were held by Mr. Darwin. His white robe is hooded and stained with bigotry, and his clan rallies to his godless cause with religious zeal. Watch them give a fiery defense of Darwin's blatant racism.

"Judge not, and you shall not be judged: condemn not, and you shall not be condemned: forgive, and you shall be forgiven" (Luke 6:37).

Building Huts

When I was a kid, I loved building huts. My friends and I would build them on the beach, in back yards, and in trees. It was so much fun. But even as a child I noticed that there was a problem. We would finish the hut, sit inside it, and say, "What will we do now?" There was nothing to do after the hut was finished.

As I matured, I found that adults had the same problem. They would build a house, have kids, the kids would grow up and leave, and the parents would find themselves saying, "What will we do now?" It is a simplistic and pessimistic view of life, but it's true. Life, because of its transient nature, is futile. It is like chasing the wind.

However, when a person is born again, a door opens. It is the door to the eternal. It banishes the curse of futility. I cannot express the joy that I have in knowing that when I serve God, I am tapping into the eternal.

"While we look not at the things which are seen, but at the things which are not seen: for the things which are seen are temporal; but the things which are not seen are eternal" (2 Corinthians 4:18).

PLANE SPEAKING

Two hundred years ago rational thinking folks would have mocked you if you spoke of the possibility of massive jumbo jets flying through the air filled with human beings. Any sensible person knew that massively heavy objects couldn't possibly fly through the air, as though they were lighter than a feather. They knew this because of an invisible law—the law of gravity. But we now know that it is possible for this to take place, because of another law that overrules gravity. When a certain object moves at a certain speed, it supersedes the invisible law of gravity and enters into another invisible law—the law of aerodynamics. Gravity still remains, but the heavy object breaks free from its influence.

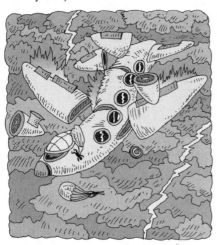

The Bible says that all of humanity is subject to an invisible law—"the law of sin and death." That law says that the soul that sins will die. Those who deny that it exists should simply take a trip to a cemetery, which they will one day. Universal death proves that this law is a reality. However, because of the Cross, the Christian breaks free from the law of sin and death. The moment he or she repents and trusts in the risen Savior, they move into the influence of another invisible law. This is a higher law—"the law of life in Christ Jesus." This is simple to prove. The skeptic needs only to step into the plane. Most don't, because of a closed mind.

"For the law of the Spirit of life in Christ Jesus has made me free from the law of sin and death" (Romans 8:2).

Interesting Thread

Matthew Wooller said, "This question raises (for me at least) the whole issue of the Rapture. Proof for the existence of God? I think that would pretty much do it for me.... According to the myth, people will vanish, the dead will rise and head off to Heaven— and we will most likely be under the control of a Jewish, homosexual, world leader.... Let us not forget that we will also get a red moon and a black sun—a huge meteor will burn one third of grass and trees—200 million horse-like creatures will run rampant; oh, and fresh water will become blood. Tell you what, if all that bunk comes to pass—I will have another think about this God thing. I can't promise anything, even then, but I will certainly have another think. Really, water turned to blood and horse-like creatures— golly."

Matthew, you may have been watching too many Hollywood movies, or the Discovery Channel, or maybe you have been reading stuff on weird websites, or eating too much cheese before you go to bed, which we know can cause bad dreams.

I would suggest that you take a deep breath, then read the Bible with a humble heart, and pray that God would show you what is prophetically symbolic and what is literal. If you don't do that, you will end up with the nightmare that you have just related. The Bible is a book filled with symbolism—from Ezekiel's wheels, to the dreams of Joseph and Daniel, to the Book of Revelation, and course, many of the words of Jesus. Again, some things are literal, and some are symbolic.

When Jesus said that He was "the Door" (see John 10:9), He didn't mean a door with literal hinges that swings back and forth. He meant that He is the entry to Heaven. (See also John 14:6.) When He said that His flesh was meat and we were to eat it, He wasn't speaking of cannibalism. We spiritually "taste and see that the Lord is good." When He held the cup of wine and said, "This is My blood" and told us to drink it, He wasn't speaking of His literal blood. He couldn't have, because His blood was still running through His veins.

Wine is often used as being symbolic of blood—turning the water into wine at the wedding in Cana, and water being turned into blood during the plagues of Egypt. All these have hidden and wonderful meanings behind them for those who are willing to dig a little. If you think about it, things that we value in life usually have to be searched out—gold doesn't lie on top of the ground. You have to search for it. It's the same with silver, diamonds, pearls, and with Bible gems. You have to dig a little to find the riches.

As much as I would like to be, I am not a prophecy expert or even a prophecy buff. I don't get too deeply into it, because so many people end up with weird and strange scenarios, and what's more, they all think that they have it right. I prefer to put my time into trying to reach people like you with the gospel. Your salvation is infinitely more important to me than my eschatological interpretation.

"Then said Jesus to them again, Verily, verily, I say to you, I am the door of the sheep" (John 10:7).

TOM'S CRUISE

The erroneous message of modern evangelism—that Jesus gives peace and happiness—has another rival. This time it's a big one. Tom Cruise said of Scientology, "We are the authorities on getting people off drugs. We are the authorities on the mind. We are the authorities on improving conditions. We can rehabilitate criminals, [show the] way to happiness. We can bring peace." The promise is that if you get on board, you can have your best life right now, by being part of their "religion,"

a religion that ironically has nothing to do with God.

Does Scientology deliver happiness and peace? Those who believe that Jesus came to give us happiness will be quick to say, as I did for years, that the world can't give *true* happiness. Even though that's what I preached, in reality, I was going through trials, temptations, and persecutions that I never experienced as a happy, peace-filled, non-Christian. There was a time when I found myself in such a deep wilderness experience that I was in absolute despair.

The truth is that Jesus didn't come to give happiness; he came to give us righteousness. The difference between the two is life and death.

"Blessed are they which do hunger and thirst after righteousness: for they shall be filled" (Matthew 5:6).

THIS IS VERY STRANGE

There was a group of people who were born blind. One of their leaders planned to take the entire group into an area in which there was a dangerous ditch that had a huge drop into fast-moving water. It was such a death trap that authorities had placed a red light in front of it, warning people not to go near the crumbling edge. When the blind men were told of the light, they wouldn't listen. They laughed instead, and mockingly said that there was no such thing as a red light. They became confirmed in their error when they cynically asked for a description of it. But no one could describe the color red to someone who was born blind.

Then came one of the reasons for their cynicism. One of them testified adamantly that he pretended for nineteen years that red did exist. He even taught others about the color and wrote songs about it. Maybe he liked being the center of attention, or maybe he did it for the money. He was totally blind, and yet he was able to fake it for all those years, which was very strange.

What was even stranger was that these blind men decided to meet regularly, and they became so fanatical about their belief—that there's no such thing as red, that they tried to censor anyone, including schoolchildren, from believing in it. And all this was done in the name of freedom and intelligence. Very strange.

They truly are the blind leading the blind.

"But if our gospel be hid, it is hid to them that are lost: in whom the god of this world has blinded the minds of them which believe not, lest the light of the glorious gospel of Christ, who is the image of God, should shine to them" (2 Corinthians 4:3-4).

ATHEISTS EVOLVED
FROM CHICKENS

A loving Christian brother emailed me and said, "Man-o-man. There are some bitter, furious, Christian-hatin' bloggers out there!" I told him that he is seeing the comparatively nice ones. They know that I delete anything with blasphemy or cussing from my blog. He's right though. Some of the atheists that contact my blog are pretty nasty. So I have decided to return a bit of the fire—in love, of course.

My new theory is that perhaps atheists evolved from the chicken because they not only have chicken characteristics—a head, eyes, mouth, skin, neck, heart, ear lobes, and legs (homology structures), but they also have the chicken's tendencies—they are chicken- livered. They hang around Christians like annoying little bugs hang around lights, trying to inject their poison whenever they can.

If you are an atheist, I hope I'm ruffling your feathers. I want to get under your skin and ask why you don't have the courage to even whisper to Muslims what you keep shouting at Christians. Prove me wrong. Get onto a Muslim website and tell them that you don't believe their god exists. Do your little "I don't believe in Zeus" thing. Tell them they believe a myth. Make sure you use the words "fairy tale." Talk about Mohammed as you do Jesus, and use your usual lower case for Mohammed. Do your "I don't believe in the flying spaghetti monster" thing. Tell them that you believe that they weren't created by (a) god, but that they evolved from primates. That should go down well.

Explain that you think they are blind simpletons to believe the way they do, and that even though there is a creation, you don't see any evidence that there is a Creator. Let them know that you think that it is intelligent to believe the way you do. You may as well explain that even though you don't believe in God's existence, you use His name as a cuss word, because you think it's worthless. Also, let them know, in no uncertain terms, that you believe that the Koran is full of mistakes (give some examples), and that their mosques are full of hypocrites.

You wouldn't dare, because you are chicken-livered. You know that they are not like Christians. Despite the anonymity of your little chicken coop, they would come after you and lop off your head. And when they found you, you would fall on your knees and be praying to God for help, quicker than I can swat a fly—and I'm pretty quick. So, think about what you are doing, and think about how much you value your life. Then think about what we are telling you. Think.

"Blessed is the man that walks not in the counsel of the ungodly, nor stands in the way of sinners, nor sits in the seat of the scornful" (Psalm 1:1).

THE HARMONY OF THE GOSPELS

I noticed that a skeptic recently mocked the Bible, challenging someone to make sense of the gospel accounts of the Resurrection. Let me quote from *The Evidence Bible*: "Both Matthew and Mark list women as the first to see the resurrected Christ. Mark says, 'He appeared first to Mary Magdalene' (Mark 16:9). But Paul lists Peter (Cephas) as the first one to see Christ after His resurrection (1 Corinthians 15:5). Jesus appeared first to Mary Magdalene, then to the other women,

and then to Peter. Paul was not giving a complete list, but only the important one for his purpose. Since only men's testimonies were considered legal or official in the first century, it is understandable that the apostle would not list the women as witnesses in his defense of the Resurrection here. The order of the appearances of Christ is as follows:

1. Mary: John 20:10–18
2. Mary and the other women: Matthew 28:1–10
3. Peter: 1 Corinthians 15:5
4. Two disciples: Luke 24:13–35
5. Ten apostles: Luke 24:36–49; John 20:19–23
6. Eleven apostles: John 20:24–31
7. Seven apostles: John 21
8. All apostles: Matthew 28:16–20; Mark 16:14–18
9. 500 brethren: 1 Corinthians 15:6
10. James: 1 Corinthians 15:7
11. All apostles: Acts 1:4–8
12. Paul: Acts 9:1–9; 1 Corinthians 15:8

Now that it makes sense to our skeptic, he will be quick to repent and trust the Savior. Yeah, right.

"And he said to them, Be not fearful: You seek Jesus of Nazareth, which was crucified: he is risen; he is not here: behold the place where they laid him" (Mark 16:6).

LOADED GUNN

A fifty-two-year-old man was arrested and his lawn mower impounded after driving down the street in Dargaville, New Zealand. Richard Gunn, who had previously lost his driver's license, had an alcohol level of more than twice the legal limit for drivers, police said. Gunn said he has been using the lawn mower to get around town since losing his license. "I thought I was safe," he told TV-One News. "Even bicycles went faster than the lawn mower's five m.p.h.," he said. "I've watched them go past me."

I am sure that the courts will take into account the type of vehicle Gunn was driving. If you were the judge, would you think that this was just a man driving a lawn mower who didn't think too deeply? Or was he a rebellious, irresponsible drunk, who totally disregarded the law, and could have run over and killed a child? That is the job of the judge—to make the right judgment, once all the evidence is in.

This brings up an important point that is often leveled at us by skeptics. They maintain that God is unjust because He is going to throw that sweet, little old lady into hell, along with Adolph Hitler. Not so. Everyone will get exactly what he or she deserves. It's called *equity* in Scripture. The Bible uses words like "greater damnation" for certain people. Whatever happens on that terrible Day will be absolute and perfect justice, given fairly to those who are guilty. No more. No less.

"Does God pervert judgment? Or does the Almighty pervert justice?" (Job 8:3).

Open-air Preaching

Rebecca said, "First, I am not a feminist, so that does not motivate the question. It is more about my looking for a way out of such a responsibility. Do women ever do open-air preaching? I've never seen it. Call me a coward, but I just can't imagine doing it, since (grateful for an excuse) I have my four-year-old in tow wherever I go. It's a terrifying thought to get up and have people heckle me. I have a desire to share the gospel, just not that way."

Rebecca, I appreciate your honesty. Yes, women do open-air preach, and it's wonderful. Two of the girls from our staff do it regularly. Here's a thought: I'm sure you would agree that sharing the gospel with someone who is prepared to listen is like giving a starving person life-giving food. Imagine having two people listen to what you have to say. Now imagine 200 people listening to every word and hearing how they can find everlasting life. That's open-air preaching on a good day.

Let me tell you two secrets about fear and preaching in the open air. First, the fear is only there *before* you preach. It's like standing beside an unheated swimming pool on a hot day. The longer you stand there, the harder it becomes to dive in. You simply have to take the plunge, and when you do, there is the initial chill to the flesh, but then it automatically adjusts, and you are swimming.

That's also what happens when you dive in and preach. When you see others dive in and see them swimming, it will give you courage. The second point is about hecklers. This is going to sound weird, but your fear of hecklers will disappear the moment you get a good one. That is the best thing that could ever happen, because they will double your listeners and sharpen your mind. Once you have had one, you will dread getting up to preach and *not* get one. Why? Because every question they come up with is old hat. There really is nothing new under the sun.

We have a DVD called *Open Air Preaching—Four in One* where you can actually see all this in action, and get teaching on the subject. Here's the blurb: "See Comfort as he takes a team from David Wilkerson's church and open air preaches in Washington Square, New York, right in the middle of a Hare Krishna convention. Witness an encounter with the New York police, learn how to draw a crowd using a fake funeral, and discover how to handle 'hecklers.' Then go step-by-step though open air preaching at UCLA and other Southern California universities. Also join Ray and his team as they preach open air in Paris, Jerusalem, London, Tokyo, Santa Monica, New Zealand, and Amsterdam."

It was seeing the New York open-air preaching video that caused Kirk Cameron to contact me and to get involved in this ministry. (For details see: www.livingwaters.com/Merchant2/merchant.mv?Screen=PROD&Product_Code=620&Category_Code=DVDs).

> *"Go therefore, and teach all nations, baptizing them in the name of the Father, and of the Son, and of the Holy Spirit"* (Matthew 28:19).

THE ABUNDANT LIFE

We live in a time that has been called "Christianity-light." The word "light" in this context means "without substance." The principles taught from these lightweight pulpits lack evangelistic punch, and instead are designed to help people make it through the struggles of this life. The hearers learn that there is a better way of living than that of the world. The fruit of this is that there is little difference between the moral lifestyles of the world and those who profess godliness.

Jesus didn't come to bring us a better life. Those who advocate that He did will be quick to point to John 10:10, in which He said that He came to bring us life, and life "more abundantly." The word "abundant" doesn't mean better, richer, and happier. It simply means life in its fullness. And if you study the life of the Apostle Paul, you will find that it was full. It was full of trials, tribulations, temptations, and persecutions. He was hated, beaten, mocked, whipped, stoned, imprisoned, and finally he was martyred. He told Timothy that all who live godly in Christ Jesus shall suffer persecution. So, what's the point in being a Christian? Why live godly in Christ Jesus if that's what you get?

It's like being in a plane that is going to crash soon, and you have a parachute on because you know that you'll have to jump 10,000 feet at any moment. The flight may get bumpy and the passengers may mock you, but who cares? What you are temporarily going through is nothing compared to their fate. So is your goal to enjoy the flight? Of course not. You want to encourage the other passengers to put their parachutes on before it's too late. You can't live with the thought of what is going to happen to them.

Listen to the wonderful words of the beloved, and much hated Prince of Preachers, Charles Spurgeon: "If by excessive labor we die before reaching the average age of man, worn out in the Master's service, then glory be to God. We shall have so much less of Earth and so much more of Heaven. It is our duty and our privilege to exhaust our lives for Jesus. We are not to be living specimens of men in fine preservation, but living sacrifices, whose lot is to be consumed."

"Yes, and all that will live godly in Christ Jesus shall suffer persecution" (2 Timothy 3:12).

Toying With Truth

I was alone in our house when suddenly I heard strange voices. They were too loud to be coming from any of the neighbors' houses, but they weren't loud enough to be understandable. It didn't make sense. Who was in our house? I stopped working on my laptop and listened closely. The voices were still unintelligible. Then I listened again. This time it was clear what was being said. I distinctly heard "e, i, e, i, o." It was Old MacDonald and his noisy farm. For some reason, one of the toys in the grandkid's playroom had decided to do its thing.

We are reasoning beings, and it's frustrating when something happens and we can't explain it. I was once frustrated with the meaning of life. It happened, and I couldn't explain it. Happy though I was, I needed more than a nebulous theory regarding our origins. I wanted to know the truth.

On April 25, 1972, I discovered the truth. I found that "In the beginning God created ..." The Creator spoke. He said, "Let there be light." And that light is still available to those who come out of the darkness. From the moment you hear His voice, you will know the truth. The Christian doesn't have a million voices telling him a thousand different things. We have One voice, and that's enough. The mystery is solved.

"Who has delivered us from the power of darkness, and has translated us into the kingdom of his dear Son" (Colossians 1:13).

Something for Atheists to Think About

A personal note to all the atheists who seem to hang around the Light: I moderate my blog myself, and I have watched with amazement as patient Christians have lovingly answered your predictable objections. I have let most of your comments through in the hope that you may soften your hearts and listen. However, by the proud way most of you talk, that doesn't seem likely.

We don't need to prove anything to you about Christianity. We are very secure in our faith, because it is not founded on a belief, but on the immovable Rock of Ages—Jesus Christ, before whom you will bow your knee.

The reason we respond to you is because we are deeply concerned about where you will spend eternity, even if you are not. Here's the bottom line: If you have lied and stolen anything, you are a lying thief. Jesus said, "Whoever looks upon a woman to lust after her has committed adultery already with her in his heart." If you hate someone, the Bible says you are a murderer, and you have to face God on Judgment Day, whether you believe in Him or not. This is why you need a Savior—"All liars will have their part in the lake of fire."

Adulterers, thieves, and fornicators (those who have sex out of marriage) will not inherit the Kingdom of God. We don't want you to end up in hell, a place that does exist. The wrath of God came upon the Savior so that it wouldn't have to come upon you. If you refuse God's offer of mercy, He will give you justice, and that is a fearful thing. Please repent and trust in Jesus today before death comes for you. Humble yourself and seek the truth. You don't need us to show it to you. You have enough light, so seek the Lord while He may be found. Thank you for reading this. Please know that there are many people praying for you.

Those who say that Christianity is a guilt trip are correct. It is a guilt trip to the foot of a bloodstained Cross, where the guilt is removed.

"Ask, and it shall be given you; seek, and you shall find; knock, and it shall be opened to you" (Matthew 7:7).

Stubborn as a Mule

My friend Scotty, his wife, Carol, and I were setting up to preach the gospel in our usual spot at Huntington Beach. It was a warm Saturday afternoon, with a lot of people milling around. As we were doing so, a street performer, who ate fire and hammered nails into his nose (a hard act to follow), came across for a friendly chat. He smiled as he suggested that we wait until he had finished his act before we spoke. He said it was in our best interest. I wasn't too happy to do that, but he said that he would only be fifteen minutes, maybe twenty, and that we could preach after he had finished. I knew that he

had a much longer act, so I told him that I would think about it. He was very congenial, friendly, kind, and very accommodating. He just wanted the best for us and for him.

After he left, I suggested that we pray about the situation. We didn't want to upset him, but we didn't want to stand there for an hour, waiting for him to finish. We didn't have an *act*, but the message of everlasting life.

After we prayed, I walked over to my kind and accommodating friend. As I approached him, I said, "We have decided to give you twenty minutes, and then we will begin." His facial expression changed. He gritted his teeth and hissed, "Don't you tell me what to do!" Then he railed at me. Suddenly, I saw that I was dealing with more than just flesh and blood. Fire didn't just go *into* his mouth.

We went ahead and preached. Our fire-eating, nose-nailing friend had his crowd, and we had ours. It was a good day, and many heard the words of everlasting life.

It's so easy to forget that our battle is not against flesh and blood, but against principalities, against powers, and spiritual wickedness in high places. It's against a subtle demonic world. Be careful to never allow anyone to stop you from sharing your faith, no matter how nice and reasonable they may be. Shake off their subtle poison, and read the Book of Acts. See how the disciples refused to obey those who tried to stop their voices. Stay in righteousness, be loving, be kind, be as gentle as a dove, and as stubborn as a mule. Be lowly of heart, be obstinate in purpose, and carry Jesus of Nazareth to the unsaved. Listen to His voice, not the voice of the crowd. They will cry "Hosanna" one moment, and "Crucify Him" the next.

> *"For we wrestle not against flesh and blood, but against principalities, against powers, against the rulers of the darkness of this world, against spiritual wickedness in high places"* (Ephesians 6:12).

My Dumb Inventions

I can't claim that I invented the poor man's remote. Back in the 1970's, there may have been other poor men who did what I did. I took some fishing tackle and strung it up the wall of the living room, along the ceiling, and down to our TV set, where I hooked it to the channel-changer and volume switch. Needless to say, I have a very tolerant wife. With a mere pull of the tackle, I could adjust the volume and change the channel without getting out of my chair.

I also gave some serious thought to the tragedy of kids drowning in swimming pools. My potential invention was a belt that children would wear any time they were around a pool. It would automatically inflate when it came into contact with water. There was one problem: if the child was heavier above the water, it could turn him upside down. I dropped that one.

Then there was the "Airbag T-shirts." They wouldn't work, because annoying people would hit the wearer on the chest.

I did have an idea that would stop cars from having head-on collisions. It was the V- shaped front and rear bumpers. These would protrude at least ten feet in the front and at the rear into sharp points, so that two cars that had them fitted could not have a head-on collision, even if they wanted to. There were a couple of problems with this idea, however. Parking wouldn't be easy, and rear-ending a car that had not been fitted wouldn't be a nice sight. Side-on collisions would be a problem, too.

Then there was my digital-clock-combination-smoke-detector. The user would know that his battery went dead because his clock stopped running. That would be a lifesaver.

Millions are laid off from work because they have bad backs from lifting. My belt buckle that snapped down into an "L" shape fixed that. When a worker picked up a heavy box, he would attach it onto the clipped-down belt buckle. This would result in straightening rather than bending of the spine.

There was also the grass-green paint, mixed with a flexible rubber, so that it could be sprayed onto lawns. The lawn would die when it was sprayed, but it would stay the same length. This would result in two things. First, no one would ever have to mow another lawn. And the second would be that I would be murdered by professional gardeners, lawn mower manufacturers, and lawn mower salesmen.

"For I am not ashamed of the gospel of Christ; for it is the power of God to salvation to every one that believes; to the Jew first, and also to the Greek" (Romans 1:18).

"I HAVE KNOWN WHAT IT IS TO USE UP ALL MY AMMUNITION, AND THEN I HAVE, AS IT WERE, RAMMED MYSELF INTO THE GREAT GOSPEL GUN AND FIRED MYSELF AT THE HEARERS — ALL MY EXPERIENCE OF GOD'S GOODNESS, ALL MY CONSCIOUSNESS OF SIN, AND ALL MY SENSE OF THE POWER OF THE GOSPEL."
CHARLES SPURGEON

From
Spurgeon Gold

THE SMELL

No one smells like a smoker. It's true, and what's more, they don't realize how bad they smell. The reason they can't perceive the same smells we do is that they have deadened the sensitivity of their noses. They literally can't smell the smells that a non-smoker can.

The conscience is like a nose. It sniffs out the stench of sin. Someone who has deadened the sensitivity of his conscience literally cannot detect how morally bad he is. That is why we need God's Law. It stirs the conscience so that it can detect sin. When the conscience does its bloodhound duty, it shows us that we don't smell like a rose, but that even our very best deeds stink (for want of a better word) to high Heaven. Check out Isaiah 64:6 and Romans 3:10-20 to sniff out more details.

"Now the Spirit speaks expressly, that in the latter times some shall depart from the faith, giving heed to seducing spirits, and doctrines of devils; speaking lies in hypocrisy; having their conscience seared with a hot iron" (1 Timothy 4:1-2).

I Don't Believe in Zeus or Mother Nature

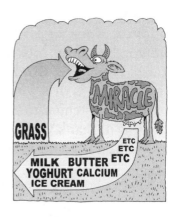

As I daily gather my chicken's eggs, I usually mumble, "Thank you, ladies." But I am not really thanking the dumb birds. I am thanking God. I go to the Source. I also thank Him for the miracle of milk. Cows just eat the grass, and it miraculously turns into milk. If you don't think it's miraculous, try turning green grass into white milk without one of God's animals. Then try turning the white milk you have made out of green grass into yellow butter, ice cream, yoghurt, and cheese. The next time you lick an ice cream cone, think about how good God is to give us those things.

I also thank Him for little green apples and big red apples. I don't thank the dirt that nurtured them. There's no such person as Mother Earth or Mother Nature. They exist only in the imaginations of the godless. Nature has no idea what it is doing when it produces trees that give us oranges, apricots, lemons, bananas, pears, and nuts; or plants that give us tomatoes, grapes, and a million different flowers. How wonderful it is of God, to give us those things. Knowing Him enriches creation. It becomes an expression of His great love and His infinite genius. How shallow and empty are the minds and existences of those who do not see God in everything. Albert Einstein was right when he said, "There are only two ways to live your life. One is as though nothing is a miracle. The other is as though everything is a miracle."

"The heavens declare the glory of God; and the firmament shows his handiwork" (Psalm 19:1).

AMERICAN PIE

How music savvy are you? Do you know the words to the famous song, "American Pie"? Sing along: "Did you write the Book of Love? Do you have faith in God above? Do you believe in rock and roll? Can music save your mortal soul?" Interesting words. One of the virtues of being made in God's image is that we can appreciate good music. No doubt you enjoy listening to a catchy tune, but have you ever taken the time to thank God for the fact that you're not deaf? To be able to hear is an unspeakable blessing.

Do you love the vivid colors of flowers and birds on this amazing planet on which we live? Then thank God that you can feast your eyes on all this color. Count your blessings. Thank Him that you are not blind. If you suddenly go blind, science can't do a thing for you. It hasn't a clue about how to even begin to make an eye. Where do you start? What would you use? Where do you gather the 137,000,000 light-sensitive cells? How do you make focusing muscles that move 100,000 times a day?

Do you enjoy good food? Then thank God that you are not starving to death in some African country, lying on the ground with flies crawling across your face. God has been good to you. He hasn't dealt with you according to your sins. We can read, think, feel, and love, and it is a sad fact of human nature that familiarity does breed contempt. We don't know what we've got until it's gone. The truth is that most of us have been given a generous slice of the American pie.

Do you love life? Then thank God that you haven't yet died in your sins and been damned from all of His future goodness. It is not too late for you to repent and trust the Savior. And make sure you don't fall into the trap of superficial thanksgiving. Thanksgiving without obedience to God is nothing but empty

> NEVER HAVE FAITH IN A MAN
> WHO HAS NO FAITH IN GOD.

hypocrisy. Prove that you are genuine in your appreciation of His goodness, by obedience to His Word. (See John 14:21 for further details.)

Now, sing along, "This could be the day that I die; this could be the day that I die ..."

"Enter into his gates with thanksgiving, and into his courts with praise: be thankful unto him, and bless his name" (Psalm 100:4).

Wrongly Named

On a summer day in 1948, a Swiss mountaineer named George de Mestral returned from a walk with his dog who was covered with burrs, the plant seed-sacs that cling to animal fur in order to travel to fertile new planting grounds. He put a burr under a microscope, and saw an amazing sight—small hooks that enabled the seed-bearing burr to cling to the tiny loops in the fabric of his pants. He realized that they were intelligently designed, and soon after George invented "Velcro" (a combination of the words *velour* and *crochet*). He should have called it "Copy-God." Instead, Velcro was patented in 1955. The rest is history.

"What is man, that you are mindful of him? and the son of man, that you visit him?" (Psalm 8:4).

Interesting Thread

Captain Howdy said, "Ray, here are examples of failed prophesies: 'When they persecute you in one town, flee to the next; for truly I tell you, you will not have gone through all the towns of Israel before the Son of Man comes' (Matthew 10:23). 'Truly I tell you, there are some standing here who will not taste death until they see that the kingdom of God has come with power' (Mark 9:1). All failed prophecies."

The key here is the word "power" (in the verse you quoted from Mark 9:1). The Kingdom of God came with power on the Day of Pentecost (see Acts 1:8). Remember, there are a spiritual kingdom (see John 3:3) and a literal kingdom, the one that will be set up on Earth by God himself. You are greatly mistaken when you say that they are failed prophecies. You know neither the Scriptures, nor the power of God.

"And what is the exceeding greatness of his power toward us who believe, according to the working of his mighty power" (Ephesians 1:19).

Unholy Huddle

Early in 2008, a couple was snowboarding in New Mexico when they became lost in a snowstorm. They had a cell phone to call for help, but decided not to use it because they were experienced hikers. They believed that they could save themselves. They built a snow hut and spent the night huddled together in the freezing conditions. The next morning they realized they were not going to be able to make it alone, so they called for help and carved an SOS in the snow. Had they not forsaken their own efforts, they certainly would have perished.

Most of humanity huddles together in this cold world, thinking that they are going to save themselves. They trust in their own religious good works. It is only when they realize that their hope of saving themselves is hopeless, that they will humble themselves and call upon the name of the Lord. May God help them to understand this, and that time is running out.

"God resists the proud, and gives grace to the humble" (1 Peter 5:5).

Another Wild Idea

I guess that one of the reasons God made flowers was to get men off the hook with women. Many times I have done or said something dumb and been able to redeem myself with a rose from the garden and a sincere note of apology. I love sending flowers to loved ones or to someone I want to encourage. However, the cost often hits me as hard in the conscience as it does in the wallet. I think of how many meals I could buy for a

starving child with the same amount of money. If a flower company had an option called "Flowers for Food," I would take that option. Instead of the recipient getting a sixty-dollar bunch of flowers, she would get one beautiful rose and a quality card that said, "This rose is a token of my deep love for you. I actually paid for a dozen roses for you, but only one was sent. This is because 75 percent of the money spent on the flowers was sent to the Children's Hunger Fund, a reputable organization that spends 99 percent of its donations on starving children. I thought this would give you more joy than eleven additional roses."

"Give, and it shall be given to you; good measure, pressed down, and shaken together, and running over, shall men give into your bosom. For with the same measure that you mete withal it shall be measured to you again" (Luke 6:38).

THE WHISTLER

I was sitting with one of my graphic artists in front of his high-tech computer when I heard a strange sound. It was like a very faint whistle. I asked if he could hear it. He stopped what he was doing for a moment and listened. He couldn't detect the sound, and so we went back to that on which we were working. A moment later I said, "There it goes again! It's a very faint whistle. Listen." He stopped working and in the stillness, both of us listened intently. No whistle. So we went back to work. Then I heard it again! It definitely was a very faint whistling sound. I said, "There it is again! It could be your computer." He stopped working for the third time (he's a very patient man), and once again, in the absolute stillness we listened intently. Then, after about fifteen seconds of dead silence, he heard it. He had a cold and his blocked nose was making a slight whistle as he breathed. Duh. We were both slightly embarrassed.

"Be still, and know that I am God" (Psalm 46:10).

THE ATHEIST VIDEO

We have a new video coming out very soon. It is called "Dinner With 40 Atheists." When it was finished being edited, someone in my office asked who had edited it. The short conversation sparked a lot of laughter. It went like this: "Who edited it? Ed edited it." Try saying that a couple of times while you are eating tomato soup. After we all tried saying, "Ed edited it" a few times, I told them who actually did  edit it. Ed didn't edit it. I was just kidding. It was Duane. He edited it. He is the brilliant director and producer of "The Way of the Master" television series. So if you feel like your mouth may not work when it comes to witnessing to atheists, this educational edifying edition will give you the edge.

"He that is of a merry heart has a continual feast" (Proverbs 15:15).

 EVEN THE INTRICACIES OF THE BRAIN OF AN ATHEIST SHOULD BE ENOUGH EVIDENCE TO PROVE THE EXISTENCE OF GOD.

WITNESSING TO WITNESSES

How do you witness to a Jehovah's Witness? Simply say this: "I have a knife in my back, and I am dying. I have three minutes to live. How can I enter the Kingdom?" Then listen to what he says. He will be thrown into frenzy, because his religion is based on works (as opposed to the biblical truth that salvation is a gift; see Romans 6:23). A Jehovah's Witness must *do* things to be saved, and that scenario exposes his motives—he is trusting in *self*-righteousness. From there, ask if he thinks that he is a good person. He will more than likely say that he thinks he is. The reason for this is because his self-righteous efforts reveal it. He knows that he is a sinner, but he believes that his sin isn't so bad that he can't earn his own way out of it and merit Heaven.

So you have to walk him through the Ten Commandments to show him that what he is trying to do is impossible. The small leap he is trying to make is over a gigantic chasm. To be saved, he first must understand that God is perfect and holy; that He considers lust to be adultery, hatred to be murder, and He will see to it that absolute justice is done. That means that adulterers, murderers, liars, and thieves will be damned forever. Once a person sees that he is a Law-breaker—a criminal who is trying to bribe the Judge of the universe with his good works— hopefully, he will trust in God's mercy alone to save him. That's how the thief on the cross was saved—through mercy alone. He didn't do anything to be saved. He couldn't go door-to-door or do good works. He couldn't, because he was nailed to a cross. That's what God's Law does to us. It nails us because of our guilt. The only thing we can do is turn to Jesus on the Cross, and say, "Lord, remember me." And even that ability to turn to Him is given to us by God. He "gives repentance to the acknowledging of the truth." (See 1 Timothy 2:25-26.) We are saved "By grace, through faith, and that not of ourselves; it is the gift of God, not of works, lest any man should boast" (Ephesians 2:8-9). So plant that seed in the hearts of those who think they can be saved by their own works, and then pray that God causes it to grow and produce fruit.

"Help me, O Lord my God: O save me according to your mercy" (Psalm 109:26).

THE POWER OF NOT BELIEVING

I am reading a book at the moment that was written by a very well-known American Christian. He talks about God helping him to give his best to everything to which he puts his hand. He's a real winner. He meets Hollywood celebrities, sports stars, and famous politicians on almost every page, and they all love and respect him. But not once does he say that he shared the gospel with them. Didn't it enter his mind to ask where these folk will spend eternity if they die in their sins? Doesn't he care? Doesn't he read the Bible? Doesn't he believe its words? This is the tragedy of contemporary Christianity. What a contrast to the Book of Acts.

"For I am not ashamed of the gospel of Christ, for it is the power of God to salvation to every one that believes; to the Jew first, and also to the Greek" (Romans 1:16).

FOR CHRISTIAN EYES ONLY

We are never as arrogant as when we are young. We think that we are invincible. However, the sad realities of life tend to humble such haughtiness. Add atheism to youth and you have a Molotov cocktail. The Bible says in 2 Peter 2:1 that there is a category of people who will depart from the faith (false converts) and end up "denying the Lord that bought them." These are in the Judas category. They look and act like disciples of Christ, and, like Judas, they may be so trusted that they even look after the church finances. But time is the test. Like Judas, they eventually sell out for the world. Temptation exposes them. The scary thing for these people is that they have God's promise (in 2 Peter 2:1) that they will be swiftly destroyed. If you don't think God would do such a thing, read Genesis 38, and see how He killed a man because He did not like what he did sexually. Or read in the Book of Acts how God killed a husband and wife simply because they told one lie. God is holy and His patience is not everlasting. So, if you are in the Judas category (and you read this when I suggested that you shouldn't), make sure you look three ways before you cross the road.

"But there were false prophets also among the people, even as there shall be false teachers among you, who privately shall bring in damnable heresies, even denying the Lord that bought them, and bring upon themselves swift destruction" (2 Peter 2:1).

Eggshell Face

Experts tell us that most deaths from sky diving happen because of human error, insinuating that if you are careful, you will be okay. Duh. Most premature deaths are from human error. Human error comes into play with car accidents, drug overdoses, pedestrian deaths, falls down stairs, medical mistakes, and on it goes. There is a reason that the *Dummies* series of books sell so well. We are crash dummies that are prone to error. Just read blogs for a few moments, and you will see what I mean. Despite careful checking, typos and wrong words sneak through. None of us is inflammable ... er ... *infallible*.

Experts think that when twenty-one-year-old Shana Richardson, on her first accelerated free-fall, jumped from 10,000 feet, she made a mistake. She began to spin out of control and ended up hitting the ground face first at fifty m.p.h. She was "egg-shelled," and ended up with fifteen metal plates in her face. So, think twice before you risk your most precious possession for a quick thrill. If you are bored with life and you need an adrenalin rush, try open-air preaching. It's more dangerous than sky diving (see Acts 7:57-60), arguably scarier, and infinitely more productive. And if your life is taken from you while you are preaching, at least your death will not be from human error. It will rather be by divine permission.

"Preach the word; be instant in season, out of season; reprove, rebuke, exhort with all longsuffering and doctrine" (2 Timothy 4:2)

Be Wise

One key to good health is to check the genetic makeup of your ancestors. Did your great-grandmother have problems with diabetes or osteoporosis? Then adjust your sugar and calcium intake accordingly. Did your great-grandfather die of heart disease? Then lay off too much fat and get plenty of exercise. Find the potential problem, and then work toward its avoidance. That's what I did when I was twenty-two years old. I looked at my ancestors and saw that they had all died. All of them. So I began to see if there was any way for the potential problem of death to be avoided.

First, I found the cause of death, which is something the scientific community couldn't figure out. It is a terminal genetic disease called *inherited sin*. Then, to my utter amazement and by the grace of God, I discovered the cure—repentance toward God and implicit trust in Jesus Christ. After all these years, that amazement is still there.

A wise man once said that when he became a Christian, he gave up that which he could not keep (his temporal life), to gain that which he could not lose (the eternal life of God in him). Be wise; give up your life. Surrender it to God, and put your trust in the Savior. If you are genuine in your commitment to Him, you will never look back, and you will never regret it. Not for a milli-second ... and you will live in eternal amazement.

"These things have I written to you that believe on the name of the Son of God; that you may know that you have eternal life, and that you may believe on the name of the Son of God" (1 John 5:13).

Myth Blown Apart

Do you know much about history? Okay, here's a question for you. How tall was Napoleon Bonaparte? If you said that he was very short, you are right. Sort of. After he died, his body was measured in French feet (*pieds de roi*) at 5' 2", but it was never correctly converted to the Standard English measure. In English feet, he was 5' 6 ½". So you were wrong.

The belief that Napoleon was very short is a myth. To a very short man, he was reasonably tall, but to a tall man, he was fairly short. It all depends on your perspective. These thoughts teach us two things. First, don't believe everything you read in history books as being factual, including what I have just quoted. And second, *short* and *tall* are relative, just as the words *good* and *evil* are relative terms if you don't have an absolute, unchanging moral standard by which to measure them. God has given us an unchanging measuring standard in His moral Law. Our ability to interpret that Law, and thereby determine good and evil, is the measure of our Christian maturity. (See Hebrews 5:14.) Have you come to the point of knowing what is morally right and wrong? If you are not sure, begin with the Gospel of Matthew chapter 5 and read through to chapter 7. That will give you the right perspective.

> *"But strong meat belongs to them that are of full age, even those who by reason of use have their senses exercised to discern both good and evil"* (Hebrews 5:14).

THOUGHT-PROVOKING

If there were an announcement that a massive asteroid was going to hit the Earth in one hour, what would you do with your last sixty minutes?

"And that, knowing the time, that now it is high time to awake out of sleep: for now is our salvation nearer than when we believed" (Romans 13:11).

WHERE IS GOD?

Why doesn't God show himself to humanity, so every skeptic would shut his mouth? Just one appearance would do. This was the cry of the Prophet Isaiah. (See Isaiah 64:1-2.) Moses asked God to show himself, and was told that he couldn't see Him and live. Here is why. The Bible tells us that God is light. This isn't the light with which we are familiar. It's called unapproachable light. When Saul of Tarsus was converted on the Road to Damascus, he saw the unapproachable light, and it was "above the brightness of the sun." It was so powerful that it would have blinded him permanently, but for God's healing grace.

Think for a moment about the sun. It is so powerful we can't even look at it for more than a brief moment without severely damaging our eyes. It is a massive ball of fire that is so big that this Earth would fit into its volume more than a million times. And it was created by the One who is fire. Scripture reveals, "Our God is a consuming fire." Why does the Bible use the word "consuming" here? It speaks of Him coming in a fearful, "flaming fire." Why would it say that, if God is supposed to be good and kind? For the same reason that a good and kind judge is filled with wrath toward a devious and unrepentant murderer who has raped and slit the throats of a number of innocent young girls. The judge's goodness is manifested in his anger.

God is unspeakably wrath-filled at sinful humanity, because He is holy, just, and good. That is why Moses couldn't stand in His presence. Moses was like you and me. He was a sinner—a criminal, with a desperately wicked heart. If he had stood before God, the holiness of His goodness as a flaming fire would have consumed him. Moses would have become an anvil for eternal justice. The only way he could be in the presence of the goodness of God was for him to be hidden in the cleft of a rock. Once he was sheltered in the rock, he was allowed to look at where God had been. (Read the account for yourself in Exodus 33.)

Look at this terrifying warning about the future: "... and to you who are troubled rest with us, when the Lord Jesus shall be revealed from heaven with his mighty angels, in flaming fire taking vengeance on them that know not God, and that obey not the gospel of our Lord Jesus Christ: who shall be punished with everlasting destruction from the presence of the Lord, and from the glory of his power" (2 Thessalonians 1:7-9).

When the holiness of God Almighty is manifested at the Second Coming of Jesus Christ (and, as sure as hell, it will be), every unsaved person will scream, "Why didn't you warn us!" And we will say, "We tried to warn you. Oh, how we tried. We told you that God had provided a cleft in the Rock, in which you could hide. He gave us a Savior so that we wouldn't have to perish. We wrote books about this incredibly good news. We printed millions of gospel tracts, we gave away Bibles, recorded CDs, produced television and radio programs, made DVDs, left our loved ones and the comfort of our homes, and preached until we were hoarse. We wept on our knees for you, and then pleaded with you, *but you wouldn't listen.* You argued instead about evolution and creation. You twisted our words. Your questioned our motives. You insulted our integrity, and called us liars. Now you have to face the justice of a holy God. The time has come for the villain to get what's coming to him. It is time for equity, and hell is your just reward. You have no one to blame but yourself. Your blood is on your own head."

What a fearful thing, to fall into the hands of the Living God.

"If a man abide not in me, he is cast forth as a branch, and is withered; and men gather them, and cast them into the fire, and they are burned" (John 15:6).

INTERESTING THREAD

"Hi, Ray, I grew up Christian," writes a questioner, "but have recently been struggling with the existence of an omnipresent, unconditional God. I don't feel it's as easy as a fish in the ocean. I can see my environment quite clearly, but God makes it difficult. I understand. He wants us to choose to love Him. For me, it's not a question of evolution or creation. I just have an abject fear that God doesn't exist. In your opinion, does this make me a 'false convert?' Do you struggle with doubt? Do you have any suggestions for someone like me?"

My answer: "You need not fear. Just say this to yourself: every building has a builder. You can't have a building without a builder—can you think of one? Buildings don't happen by themselves. It's impossible ("For every house is built by some man ..." Hebrews 3:4). The same principle applies to paintings and painters. The painting is absolute proof that there is a painter—try and think of a painting that didn't have a painter. Paintings don't happen by themselves. It's impossible.

Here's my point. Creation is *absolute* proof that there is a Creator. You cannot have a creation without a Creator. It is impossible. Then the question "Who made God?" has a logical answer. End of argument. Unless, according to the Bible, you are a fool. (Read Psalm 14:1 and Romans 1:20.) People on my blog often disagree with such basic logic. You try and objectively analyze why they would do such a thing. If you do that, what they say will strengthen your faith in God.

To address your other question—do I struggle with doubt? Never. I would *never* for a moment doubt the existence of God, because of the evidence of creation. I would never doubt the reality of God, because, in a moment of time, He transformed my life. And I would never doubt the character of God because I trust His integrity implicitly. The Bible says that if you doubt God, you call Him a liar. (See 1 John 5:10.) If I doubt you when you tell me something, it's an insult to your integrity. It means I think that you are a liar. So, never doubt God. Trust Him with all your heart. (See Proverbs 3:5.)

The word "atheist" contains the word "God." Those poor folk can't get away from God. The Bible says, "In Him we live and have our being." They are like fish in a large ocean, saying that there's no proof the ocean exists.

> "*Because that which may be known of God is manifest in them; for God has showed it to them*" (Romans 1:19).

Beaten by an Ex-cop

I was badly beaten recently by a retired police officer from the LA County Sheriff's Department. I fought back with everything I had, but it was no use. The man was overpowering. I never thought that this would happen to me. He had the muscle to beat people, and that's what he was doing to me. It was a nightmare. He wanted to take me down, and so he relentlessly pulverized me, hitting me again and again. He struck with his right hand, and then before I could recover, his backhand came at me. My heart pounded and sweat poured from my brow. The beating was so painfully bruising it will be some time before I recover. How I hate losing at ping pong, but Tony's more than twenty years as a police officer had instilled in him a disciplined mind and quick reflexes.

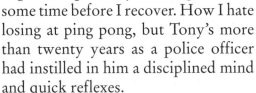

Most men have a similar competitive nature. We don't like to lose. That hard-headedness isn't so common in women, but I did speak to one young lady who said that she feared being a loser more than she feared dying. Maybe you are the same. You would hate to be called a loser. If that's true, read these words very slowly: "What shall it profit a man if he shall gain the whole world and lose his own soul?" You can't get to be a bigger loser than that. We are talking about your life, and we are talking about eternity. So stop resisting. There's no way you are going to win your battle against God, so give up the fight, and come over to the winning side.

"Whosoever will come after me, let him deny himself, and take up his cross, and follow me. For whosoever will save his life shall lose it; but whosoever shall lose his life for my sake and the gospel's, the same shall save it" (Mark 8:34-35).

WHAT IS EVIL?

After my manager and I had dinner with a group of atheists, a number of other atheists expressed surprise and considered it brave of us to enter into a "den of lions." The implication was, "Do you think that we are evil?" Well, let's do a little test to see if you are. We will call it "The Evil Test." To do it, we need a standard to see if the test has been passed. Without a standard, the test is irrelevant. We will use atheistic morality—a "nothing is absolutely right or absolutely wrong" standard.

Question # 1: Is it evil to kill a baby in the womb? Answer: The consensus is that the fetus is not human, so the answer is "No. It is not evil. It is a woman's right." 2. Is it evil to say that there is no God? Answer: "There is no proof of God's existence, so of course it's not evil to say that God doesn't exit. The thought is ridiculous." 3. Is it evil to hate someone? Answer: "No it's not." 4. Is it evil to look at pornography? Answer: "Definitely not. It's not hurting anyone, so how can it be evil? That's ridiculous. Who is to say what's right and what's wrong? Of course it's not evil."

So the atheist passes the test with flying colors, *because he judges himself by his own moral standard.* However, his "Who is to say what's right and what's wrong?" is telling. When we ask the same questions using the absolute, unchanging morality of God's Law, which *does* tell us what's right and what's wrong, there is a completely different outcome. The Bible says that even if I don't advocate abortion and atheism, or don't hate anyone or look at porn, my heart isn't just "evil," it's "desperately wicked." (See Jeremiah 17:9-10.)

When we are a "law unto ourselves," as the Bible says, we will never think that we are evil by nature. But if we have an honest look at ourselves under the light of God's unchanging Law, we will find that His testimony is true, as will be seen on Judgment Day.

There is a way which seemeth right unto a man, but the end thereof are the ways of death (Proverbs 14:12).

THE DIFFICULTY WITH FAITH

I sat next to a man on a plane, whose job was to purchase land for a well-known handyman chain store. Part of his job was to count houses in prospective areas. He wasn't interested in how many people lived in each house, because the chain store's income came from purchases for the houses, not for the people who lived in them. He said supermarket chains were the opposite. They couldn't care less how many houses were in an area, just people, because it's people that eat food, not houses. He alone carried out the whole process of negotiating the price

for the land purchases, and had been doing that same job for thirty years. He agreed with me when I said that he was in a position of great trust.

Much of what we do in life has its foundation in trust. We trust our dentist when he drills, our taxi driver when he drives, our pilots when they fly. We trust our history books, our teachers, and some still even trust politicians. Marriage is a trust relationship. So are business partnerships and friendships. We trust elevators, planes, cars, brakes, chairs, doctors, surgeons, brokers, and television anchors. This is why it's hard to understand why skeptics mock the thought of trust in God. They think that a Christian is someone who *believes* in God's existence. Rather, a Christian is someone who trusts God's promises, trusts in His integrity, and His incredible ability. When we speak of faith in Jesus, it is not an intellectual assent. It is an implicit trust in Him as our sin-bearer. So never trust anyone who says that they find it difficult to have trust or faith in God. There's nothing difficult about trust, when the One you are trusting is utterly trustworthy.

> *"It is of the Lord's mercies that we are not consumed, because his compassions fail not. They are new every morning: great is your faithfulness"* (Lamentations 3:22-23).

A Small Prediction

I am not good at predicting the future. I thought that there would be a bloodbath when Communist China took back Hong Kong some years ago. I was wrong. Most of us have been wrong about political predictions, the sex of our baby predictions, etc., so I have learned to keep my mouth shut when it comes to the subject. Almost shut—because I have one small prediction to make about you, if you are a skeptic when it comes to Christianity. I will give you a short list of some of the prophecies of the Bible, and then make my little prediction. These prophecies were written approximately 2,000 years ago, and are what are called "signs" of the end of the age. Here's the list of what the New Testament says will take place just before the Second Coming of Jesus Christ: There will be an increase in wars and hostility between nations, homosexuality, knowledge, travel, earthquakes, famines, violence, and vegetarianism. (See 1 Timothy 4:1-5, KJV. Note the word "creature.") There will also be a breakdown of the institution of marriage, an empty and dead religious system, money-hungry preachers who would have many followers and slander the name of Christianity, a forsaking of the Ten Commandments (see Matthew 24:12), and mockery of Noah's flood. (See 2 Peter 3:3-6.)

Now here's my prediction. If you are a skeptic, you will be saying, "But these signs have always been around!" To be completely honest, your saying that isn't *my* prediction. The Bible says that you would say it (2 Peter 3:4), and it even says *why* you are rebelling against the Word of God—because you are full of lust. How's that for hitting the nail on the head? The key to understanding the era in which we live is not to be ignorant of the fact that God dwells outside of the dimension of time, and that a day to Him is as a thousand years to us. Jesus said to keep your eye out for one sign: when the Jews repossessed Jerusalem that would bring all these signs into culmination. The Jews became a nation in 1948, and got Jerusalem back in 1967. They found a homeland for the first time in 2,000 years. What are you waiting for? You had better make peace with God.

> "*Therefore being justified by faith, we have peace with God through our Lord Jesus Christ*" (Romans 5:1).

GOODWILL TO ALL MEN

Someone kindly sent me a fifty-dollar voucher to a well-known clothing chain. I was excited to see their selection because they were known for their trendy clothes. When I found a gap in my time, I went to the store, but became disillusioned within minutes. They were selling jeans and shirts that looked like they had been rejected from a Goodwill store. Everything was either ripped, tattered, filled with holes, faded, torn, or wrinkled. The store's clientele consisted of vulnerable, peer-driven teenagers, who have been made to feel cool while wearing rags. Advertisers must be smiling all the way to the bank. We sure are like sheep. I gave the voucher to a friend.

"There is none that understands, there is none that seeks after God" (Romans 3:11).

What Is Reality?

In the days when Communists were called "Reds," a man named Rudolph Strauboroff and his wife were looking out of the window of their large, wooden mansion in Moscow. As he stared at the freezing conditions, he said, "It's beginning to rain." His wife quietly informed him that it was snow, not rain. He looked her in the eyes, and gently said, "Rudolph the Red knows rain, dear."

Yes, I know how bad that joke is, but it leads me to a serious question on the subject of *knowing* anything. What

do we know in this life? Of what can we be sure? To find out, I have some strange questions for you. Here's the first. When is "now?" Tell me if you can. I'm serious. Pinpoint "now." You can never pinpoint when it is, because by the time you do, it's gone. "Now" is as elusive as evidence for species-to-species evolution. In an instant it becomes "then." Here's another dumb question. Where is "here?" Point to it. If you say it's where you are, six billion others on Earth would disagree with you. "Here" is where they are, and to them, where you are pointing, is "there." Another one: Which way is "up?" If you point toward the sky, millions of folk down-under would disagree with you. If they point to the sky to show the direction of "up," they will point in the opposite direction to which you are pointing. Remember, we live on a big round ball. The same applies to the direction of "down." If you point to the soil to show the direction of "down," people on the other side of the world doing the same thing are pointing in the opposite direction, and people halfway around the world (at the equator) would be pointing in a completely different direction.

Here's another one. What color is the sky on a cloudless day? If you said "blue," you are wrong. There's no color to it. It's colorless. If you don't believe it, check it out from space. There's no "sky" at all. How about a sunrise? Have you ever seen one? No one has. The sun never "rises" or "sets." Remember, the Earth turns, while the sun just sits there. So, what can you be sure of in this life? Some say, "Death and taxes." That's not true, either—plenty of people manage to avoid taxes.

So, if we can't be sure of anything but death, what on Earth is reality (truth)? If you leave God out of the equation, you have no answer. What is truth? Is there any such thing? Do you know? Again, if you ignore Almighty God—the I AM who transcends time and space—you will end up as lost as the

---

"NO MAN WILL EVER PUT ON THE ROBE OF CHRIST'S RIGHTEOUSNESS TILL HE IS STRIPPED OF HIS FIG LEAVES, NOR WILL HE WASH IN THE FOUNT OF MERCY TILL HE PERCEIVES HIS FILTHINESS. THEREFORE, MY BRETHREN, WE MUST NOT CEASE TO DECLARE THE LAW, ITS DEMANDS, ITS THREATENINGS, AND THE SINNER'S MULTIPLIED BREACHES OF IT."
CHARLES SPURGEON

From
Spurgeon Gold

misguided Pilate in Scripture, as he stood, bewildered, in front of Jesus Christ. The Roman governor asked the rhetorical question, "What is truth?" Pilate gazed on Him who was Reality itself (see John 14:6), and you are just as close to Him. (See Romans 10:8-9.) Are you going to wash your hands of Jesus Christ like Pilate did? Or will you obey Him, and know the certainty of the words from John's Gospel, "... and you shall know the truth, and the truth shall make you free" (John 8:32)?

> *"Jesus said to him, I am the way, the truth, and the life: no man comes to the Father, but by me"* (John 14:6).

INTERESTING THREAD

John Botha said, "Well, as an ex-Christian, I can say that I was never afraid of most atheists—only the informed ones! Those are the ones who can show that the Christian belief system is full of holes.

Ray Comfort said, "Correction: false convert."

John Botha said, "Oh, Ray, correction: true convert. Why does your worldview and biblical knowledge not allow you to see that many can be Christians and then 'fall away.' It's clearly taught, you know. I understand the concept of being a false convert, but I passed the tests of a true convert that *you wrote* for many years, so maybe you need to re-write those?"

Ray Comfort said, "Not true. This is what I teach: 'And Jesus said to him, No man, having put his hand to the plough, and looking back, is fit for the kingdom of God' (Luke 9:62). If someone even looks back, he's not fit for the Kingdom. You didn't just look back; you *went* back, proving the spurious nature of your profession. Judas faked it for three-and-a- half years, and it seems you lasted longer. Time usually reveals the hypocrite, the pretender. Please try again, and this time, do it properly."

John Botha said, "Hey, Ray, I know what you teach; I have all your DVDs, CDs, tracts, etc, I even bought the t-shirt, the one with the spider. I don't want to 'try again.' You really shouldn't trivialize my experience so much. You should be more patient and understanding, as it's altogether possible that you could be wrong. The verses you quote contradict others that say people can fall away—and be restored. You said: 'You didn't just look back; you went back, proving the spurious nature of your profession.' Look, no point arguing the matter. God knows I spent enough time doing it when I was churching it. I'm happy to concede that according to, not only your view but my own, I was a 'false convert.' I must have been, not only because you say so, but also due to the fact that it's not actually possible to be a born-again Christian because the new birth, Christ, and the Holy Spirit do not actually exist. So I was a false convert believing in a false Christ and a false God. All of my experiences were in my little head. All the 'fruits' of my life, ministry, and finally the large church I pastored were all a sham. After all, there really wasn't a big change in my life. I just swapped my heathen sins for Christian ones—like pride, arrogance, gluttony, bigotry, and narrow-mindedness. Peace out."

THE MEANING OF GOODBYE

Good–bye: NOUN ETYMOLOGY: ALTERATION OF "GOD BE WITH YOU."

Ray Comfort said, "Exactly. The whole thing was a fake, from start to finish. Your words confirm the spurious nature of your experience. I don't know how you lasted so long and got so far, but America in particular is full of these empty-experience 'conversions' that are the tragic fruit of the modern gospel. I'm sorry you went through all this. If I were in your shoes, I'm sure I would be bitter."

My friend Joel said, "Ray, I have a few questions. Firstly, what do you mean by 'living God'? Are you saying that God is alive? I assume that's not what you mean, but I can't figure out what you do mean."

Mankind is prone to idolatry. Idols are anything in our affections that replace God as the Supreme Being. For example, atheism is a form of idolatry. It replaces the true and living God, the source of life, with the god of time. Time is the creative force behind evolution. Time brought everything into being. If time didn't pass its magic hand over evolution, nothing would have happened. Evolution is dead without the life of time.

"Secondly," Joel continues, "I can't puzzle out how you can so easily dismiss other religions and their gods, but find it impossible to do the same with your own. Almost all other religions have their holy books, their devoted followers, and the same certainty that they are correct and everyone else is wrong. What makes your certainty different from theirs? What makes your faith correct while theirs suffers from some obvious fallacy? Why are your arguments against the other gods and religions somehow not valid when applied to Christianity? What sets Christianity apart?"

That is a very good question. Here's the answer in a nutshell. All religions are man-made, and they are based on something called self-righteousness. They say that there are

BE CAREFUL OF LUST.
IT OFTEN MASQUERADES AS CURIOSITY.

certain things called righteous deeds that each of us must do to get to Heaven and to escape hell. Moslems say that you must pray five times a day, fast, and accept Mohammed as a prophet. Hinduism says you must do things to try and escape the hopeless spiral of reincarnation. Mormonism and Jehovah's Witnesses say essentially the same thing. They say that man's salvation is based on what he does. The reason they believe that is because they are ignorant of the standard that God requires of them. They think His standard of righteousness is the same as theirs. It's not.

God's standard is absolute perfection in thought, word, and deed. He considers lust as adultery, hatred as murder. Lying lips are an abomination to Him. He is so holy that His justice requires that all liars will have their part in the lake of fire. It is only when His Law comes into play through the Ten Commandments that we begin to understand that we are desperately wicked criminals in His sight. We are standing guilty in the courtroom of eternal justice. It is the Law that shows us that our good works, or religious deeds, are in truth, attempts to bribe the Judge of the universe, and that the catalyst of religious works is a guilty conscience, or what the Bible calls an evil conscience.

However, God will not be bribed. We are guilty criminals against God, we are Law-breakers, and we are awaiting capital punishment. But the Bible tells us that this perfect and holy Judge of the universe is "rich in mercy." If we cast ourselves on the mercy of the court, through repentance and faith in Jesus, God can dismiss our case, and let us live. He can commute our death sentence, and save us from damnation in hell. And He can do that because He paid the fine for us with the life blood of His Son. The Living God created for himself a perfect body and filled that body as a hand fills a glove. Jesus of Nazareth was the "express image of the invisible God." He came to suffer and die in our place, to take the punishment for our sins. He came to pay our fine and defeat death. That is what separates Christianity from man-made religions. This is explained a little more clearly in my booklet, *Why Christianity?* (www.livingwaters.com/Merchant2/merchant. mv?Screen=PROD&Product_Code=512)

> *"And he is before all things, and by him all things consist"* (Colossians 1:17).

Blowing Your Cover

Atheist: a´the-ist, n. [Gr. without God; priv. + God: cf. F. athéiste.], Webster's Dictionary. The word "atheist" is a revealing word. It says nothing about a *non-belief* in God. It just says that if someone professes to be an atheist, they are without God. A Christian is someone who is with God. That's why Jesus is called

WITH GOD   **WITHOUT GOD**

"Immanuel," which means "God with us." Repent of your sins and trust Jesus Christ, and instead of being *without God*, an atheist, you will be *with God*, a Christian. Cool, huh?

> *"For you are dead, and your life is hid with Christ in God"* (Colossians 3:3).

How to Get Popular

Politicians are some of the most hated people on the planet. However, the way to become almost universally admired as a politician is to be assassinated. It's tragic, but true. Think of Abraham Lincoln. His name is revered by most. Or JFK. Or think of Dr. Martin Luther King. Their deaths lifted them above the esteem of the average celebrity. In fact, death changes the most rotten husbands, the most corrupt politicians, and in general, the nastiest people into the most moral of people. It is very common for the living to say of the dead, "He was a good man." Why do we do that? Why are people spoken of differently in life than they are in death? It may be more than just a respect for the dead. It may come from a sense of self-justification.

"As it is written, There is none righteous, no, not one" (Romans 3:10).

Weak-minded Christians

I have lost count of how many times I have heard that Christianity is a crutch for weak-minded people, who can't make it in life without faith. Well, that may be, but we aren't the only ones who need to lean on something. Do you know how many people use alcohol and drugs as a crutch to get them through life, or how many people can't walk into a room without clutching onto a cigarette? According to the

Substance Abuse and Mental Health Services Administration there are 22.6 million Americans who are addicted to drugs and alcohol. Those kinds of crutches tend to snap and leave the patient in a worse state. Faith in God isn't like that. He will never let you down—in this short life or in the life to come. You can lean on Him. I don't have to be concerned with the troubles of the future, because the future with its trouble is in His hands. He's already there, and nothing takes Him by surprise. The word "crutch" is a poor metaphor for the Savior. It is more biblical to say that faith in Jesus is a like a parachute, and death is a fearful jump into eternity. You may be of the opinion that a parachute is a crutch, used by weak-minded people who can't handle the jump by themselves. If that's the case, then I am weak-minded. I need a Savior.

"For without me you can do nothing" (John 15:5).

Big News

In Connecticut, a man named Reggie Damone just wanted to jot down a phone number when he picked up what he thought was litter on a sidewalk. But what he found was an envelope containing a check for $185,000. Guess what he did? "Damone, who receives food stamps and works at McDonald's, said he didn't think twice about trying to cash it. Instead, the forty-seven-year-old took a bus from his Jewett City home to a bank and returned the check to the niece of the landlord to whom the check was written." Wow. That made national news, and so it should. Every time the media broadcast something like this on the news, they are verifying the truth of Scripture—that the

CHARLES SPURGEON SAID:

"THERE IS A WAR BETWEEN YOU AND GOD'S LAW. THE TEN COMMANDMENTS ARE AGAINST YOU. THE FIRST COMES FORWARD AND SAYS, 'LET HIM BE CURSED. FOR HE DENIES ME. HE HAS ANOTHER GOD BESIDE ME. HIS GOD IS HIS BELLY AND HE YIELDS HIS HOMAGE TO HIS LUST.'

From
Spurgeon Gold

ALL THE TEN COMMANDMENTS, LIKE TEN GREAT CANNONS, ARE POINTED AT YOU TODAY. FOR YOU HAVE BROKEN ALL OF GOD'S STATUTES AND LIVED IN DAILY NEGLECT OF ALL HIS COMMANDS. SOUL, YOU WILL FIND IT A HARD THING TO GO TO WAR WITH THE LAW. WHEN THE LAW CAME IN PEACE, SINAI WAS ALTOGETHER ON A SMOKE AND EVEN MOSES SAID, 'I EXCEEDINGLY FEAR AND QUAKE!' WHAT WILL YOU DO WHEN THE LAW OF GOD COMES IN TERROR; WHEN THE TRUMPET OF THE ARCHANGEL SHALL TEAR YOU FROM YOUR GRAVE; WHEN THE EYES OF GOD SHALL BURN THEIR WAY INTO YOUR GUILTY SOUL; WHEN THE GREAT BOOKS SHALL BE OPENED AND ALL YOUR SIN AND SHAME SHALL BE PUNISHED?...

CAN YOU STAND AGAINST AN ANGRY LAW IN THAT DAY?"

"You have heard that it was said by them of old time, You shall not commit adultery: but I say to you, that whosoever looks on a woman to lust after her has committed adultery with her already in his heart" (Matthew 5:27-28).

heart of man isn't good; it is "desperately wicked." It is big news when a human being does what is right.

> *"The heart is deceitful above all things, and desperately wicked: who can know it?"* (Jeremiah 17:9).

Questions and Objections

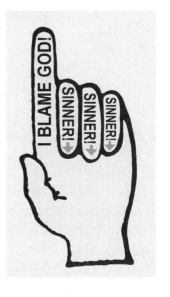

Neil H. said, "As Thomas Paine put it, rather more concisely, this was 'an order to butcher the boys, to massacre the mothers, and debauch the daughters.' There are many occasions of the Lord waxing wroth against the people of Israel, never mind the numerous tribes that they came into conflict with who were massacred or enslaved. The oddest example that springs to mind is in Exodus 32. It suggests that the Lord committed an evil act in contemplating wrath for which He only repented when Moses promised to conquer the lands on His behalf. How could He repent unless He had done something wrong in the first place?"

If you think that's bad, how about the fact that God has proclaimed the death sentence upon every man, woman, and child on the face of the Earth? It gets worse. Eternal damnation in a terrible place called hell awaits everyone who has done evil. Everyone. The day will come when absolute justice will be applied. That's wonderful news ... if you are not a criminal in God's eyes. And if His judgments upset you, here's a verse for you to think about: "The judgments of the Lord are true and righteous altogether" (Psalm 19:9). I trust Him and I am not offended at all by anything He does. You don't trust Him and you are offended. There's a reason for that. Let's talk now about your sins for a moment. Have you ever lusted after a woman? Have you lied or stolen or used God's name in vain? If you are like the rest of us and have done those things, you are a lying, thieving, blasphemous adulterer at heart. (See Matthew 5:27-28.) In light of this, who are you to stand in moral judgment over Almighty God! Delusions of grandeur, indeed. Humble yourself, Neil, and you will see things as they are.

"For whosoever shall keep the whole law, and yet offend in one point, he is guilty of all" (James 2:10).

Question and Answer

An angry atheist writes, "Welcome to a dangerous new era, the Un-Enlightenment, in which centuries of rational thought are overturned by idiots. Superstitious idiots. They're everywhere—reading horoscopes, buying homeopathic remedies, consulting psychics, babbling about 'chakras' and 'healing energies,' praying to imaginary gods, and rejecting science in favor of soft-headed bunkum. But instead of slapping these people round the face till they behave

like adults, we encourage them. We've got to respect their beliefs, apparently.... Why should your outmoded codswallop be treated with anything other than the contemptuous mockery it deserves?"

Mr. Atheist, I found myself saying a hearty "Amen" to everything you said. We are surrounded by weirdos and crazies—superstitious, simple-minded people who believe anything they are told. If the folk who write horoscopes really knew the future, they would all play blackjack, be super rich, and live in big mansions in Las Vegas and Reno. Or they would have high-paying jobs on primetime TV, telling us about tomorrow's weather. My TV co-host and I snuck into a psychic store in Hollywood with a hidden camera and tried to expose them. We got kicked out, because our questions cut too close to the bone. Yep, "Amen" to all the healing energy stuff and the soft-headed bunkum, and another "Amen" to the imaginary gods. A big "Amen" to your small "g." Man is forever making up false gods and bowing down to their image. It's crazy. Pizzas that look like Mary really turn my stomach. It is all outmoded codswallop. Right on. You're not alone. Keep preaching it. We just go one step further—stop all this nonsense; just love and serve the living God. I do make one small prediction, though, and there's nothing psychic about me. My prediction is that this statement will make you mad. Then after you read that I said it would make you mad, you will decide that it won't. Then you will be a little confused as to how to respond. Let's see if I'm right.

"For you shall worship no other god: for the Lord, whose name is Jealous, is a jealous God" (Exodus 34:14).

Beware of Wolves

I noticed that a dear Christian was going through a trying time, and a "kind" atheist gave her his two-cents worth. All he was trying to do, in the name of hugs, love, and concern for her well-being was to sow seeds of doubt about the promises of God. The woman needed to hear the exact opposite. This graphic

and typically wonderful quote from Charles Spurgeon will stir a hornet's nest, but it is applicable in this situation:

"A smooth tongue is a great evil; many have been bewitched by it. There be many human anteaters that with their long tongues covered with oily words entice and entrap the unwary and make their gain thereby. When the wolf licks the lamb, he is preparing to wet his teeth in its blood."

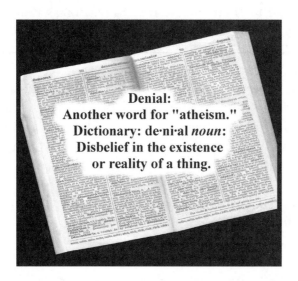

Denial:
Another word for "atheism."
Dictionary: de·ni·al *noun*:
Disbelief in the existence
or reality of a thing.

Questions and Objections

"What really shocks me here are the number of Christians who are afraid of atheists," writes one skeptic. "What is scary about someone not believing the same thing you do? Perhaps I am asking the wrong question. Perhaps I should be asking, 'Are you that afraid that your belief system is that easily deconstructed?'"

Good question. We are not scared of atheists, although if we weren't Christians, we should be. A very wise man once said, "Most I fear God. Next, I fear him who fears Him not." Atheists are probably about as dangerous as "religious" people (as opposed to those who truly love God). Religious zealots have killed millions of people throughout history in religious wars (the Crusades, Islamic terrorism, etc.), the Spanish Inquisition (the murder of infidels and heretics by the Roman Catholic Church), the killing of the prophets of God (by religious Jews), the murder of Jesus, and the

persecution of the Church. (See the Book of Acts for details, or read *Foxe: Voices of the Martyrs* for greater and horrific detail.)

Religious hypocrites come in a close second to atheistic communism, which is responsible for one hundred million deaths throughout history. If someone doesn't fear God, they will lie to you (if they think that they can get away with it), they will steal from you (if they think they can get away with it), and they may even kill you (if they … well, you know why by now). The atheist thinks that he's getting away with his sin. He denies that there is a God, and therefore he believes that there is no judgment for his actions. He may evade civil law, but there is no way he can ever evade God's Law. God considers lust to be adultery, and hatred, murder. He sees the thought life, and Jesus warned that even every idle word he speaks, he will have to give an account for on the Day of Judgment.

"The Lord knows the thoughts of man, that they are vanity" (Psalm 94:11).

RUSTY HARP

Some people think that Christians believe we are going to spend eternity sitting on a cloud playing a rusty harp. If that were all I hoped for, I wouldn't be a Christian. The hope that I have isn't nebulous. It is concrete. It's what is called an anchor of the soul. It is both sure and steadfast.

Here's what it is: think about the beauty of this massive Earth. Think of a tall, snow-covered mountain, or a clear, babbling brook, or a beautiful beach with clean, white sand, crystal-clear waters filled with an amazing array of brightly colored fish. The pristine waters reflect a sky-blue sky, and the beach is surrounded with straight, tall, and green palm trees. Think of magnificent California redwoods or of the incredible assortment of tasty fruit trees, or the breathtaking beauty of a sunrise or sunset, or the magnificence of the Grand Canyon or Niagara Falls. Got it in mind? Now think of this. All who repent and trust in Jesus Christ, whether Jew or Gentile, black or white, male or female, rich or poor—will inherit this Earth.

God has given it to us, and it will be ours for eternity. God's spiritual Kingdom came to this Earth on the Day of Pentecost, and the time will come when the literal Kingdom will come to this Earth, and the will of God will be done on Earth as it is in Heaven. We not only escape hell, but also by God's grace we get Heaven on Earth. So, if you are a Christian, make sure you know what God has in store for those that love Him, and if you are not, make sure you know what God has in store for those that hate Him.

"Which hope we have as an anchor of the soul, both sure and steadfast, and which enters into that within the veil" (Hebrews 6:19).

Bad Language

The English language is very inadequate. If I say that I "love" another man, it has perverted overtones. That's because there's only one word for love in the English language. Not so in the Greek and Hebrew, which are the languages of the Bible. I have been frustrated as to how to describe the mentality of an atheist. I could say that they are "mentally bankrupt," but that sounds  cruel and it even degenerates to abuse. Those English words are very limited in their description. However, the Hebrew does a better job. The transliteration of the Hebrew word used to describe the atheist, used in Psalm 14:1 is *nabal* (pronounced "naw-bawl"). It means a "stupid; wicked (especially impious); foolish (both male and female); vile person." That hits the mark. It shows why the atheist is a fool.

"We know that we have passed from death to life, because we love the brethren. He that loves not his brother abides in death" (1 John 3:14).

"ATHEISTS EXPRESS THEIR RAGE AGAINST GOD, ALTHOUGH IN THEIR VIEW HE DOES NOT EXIST."
C. S. LEWIS

Stupid Chickens

I have noticed something very strange about my chickens. They are bold. The moment I walk into the coop, they run toward me as though I am going to give them something. Very friendly, indeed. But the moment I reach down to pick them up or pat them, they cower like ... like chickens. They squat. Their wings go out. Then they physically tremble.

I have noticed something very strange about myself. I come before my Father in Heaven with great boldness. I am filled with expectation for His blessings. He has good things in store for believers. We have a love relationship. But the moment His hand comes upon me and I feel His guidance to witness to a stranger, I become chicken. I am serious. I have personally witnessed to thousands of people. I have preached in the open air thousands of times, and yet when I feel that God wants me to approach a stranger, I want to squat right were I am and tremble. Such stupidity in chickens and in myself makes me laugh. We are pretty pathetic. May God help us in our weaknesses.

"My grace is sufficient for you: for my strength is made perfect in weakness" (2 Corinthians 12:9).

"If you wish to know God, you must know His Word. If you wish to perceive His power, you must see how He works by His Word. If you wish to know His purpose before it comes to pass, you can only discover it by His Word."
Charles Spurgeon

From
Spurgeon Gold

Into Your Own Hands

Back in 2006, wildlife expert Steve Irwin tragically died when a barb from a stingray shot through his heart. His natural instinct was to pull it out, and experts say that is what killed him. Had he left it in and been rescued, there was a possibility that surgery could have saved his life. Dr. Eugene Costantini, who operated on eighty-two-year-old American stingray victim James Bertakis, said that Irwin might have been able to receive vital medical attention had he not ripped the barb out of his chest. "The key was the removal that released the blood flow from the inside of the heart and I think that was probably the final event for Steve … If [the barb] had been left in place, he might have had the opportunity to make it to a hospital."

The following year, 2007, was a difficult one for me. Incident after incident took place where I felt stabbed through the heart. My natural instinct was to try and justify myself. I wanted to take things into my own hands, but I didn't. I instead committed myself into the hands of the Chief Surgeon. I did so because I knew that that is God's way, and to do things His way is a lifesaver, indeed. Look at Jesus, our great example in Scripture: "Who did no sin, neither was guile found in his mouth: who, when he was reviled, reviled not again; when he suffered, he threatened not; but committed himself to him that judges righteously" (1 Peter 2:22-23). So if you are going through a tough time, and you feel like taking things into your own hands, stop and think about it for a moment. It may seem like the right thing to do, but the consequences may be tragic.

"But I say to you, Love your enemies, bless them that curse you, do good to them that hate you, and pray for them which despitefully use you, and persecute you" (Matthew 5:44).

Questions and Objections

"Here's a question for you," writes an atheist. "If a 'missing link' was discovered, or something showing that men and apes had a common ancestor, would you stop believing in God?"

To answer this question, I'm going to have to use an "ATMAM." An "ATMAM" is an acronym for an "Analogy That Makes Atheists Mad." Here goes: The question is similar to asking me, "If you discovered that your mother-in-law was a draught horse, would you stop believing that your wife existed?" The analogy is applicable because I know that it's impossible for Sue's mother to be another species (it's against nature), and I could never deny the existence of my wife because I know her.

Atheists think that a Christian is someone who *believes* that God exists. That's not true. A Christian, in the biblical sense, is someone who *knows* God experientially. This fact is almost impossible to get through to an atheist, but I will illustrate it from another angle. I believed in God's existence before I was a Christian. I wasn't dim-witted enough to look at creation and say that there was no Creator. Of course I believed in God like every other sane and reasoning human being. But on the 25th of April 1972, at 1:30 in the morning, I came to know the Lord. I moved out of the realm of belief, into the realm of experience. I know Him "whom to know is life eternal." When a sinner comes to know God it's called "conversion," or "the new birth."

"Jesus answered and said to him, Verily, verily, I say to you, Except a man be born again, he cannot see the kingdom of God" (John 3:3).

Two Difficult Words to Say

Salvation is unattainable for a proud person, because it entails the humility of saying, "I'm sorry. I was wrong." That's no easy feat for an egocentric, self-righteous person. Man's sinful pride is truly a killer. This is never so clear as in a marriage breakup. A husband or wife would rather keep their pride and lose their children. They would rather destroy their marriage than apologize. That really stinks, and I say that metaphorically.

No wonder God "resists the proud." No wonder "everyone that is proud of heart is an abomination to the Lord." However, it's interesting to note from Scripture that salvation isn't even attainable for a humble person. Even the humble need the hand of God to bring them to Christ. We may not have had the drama of a conversion like Saul of Tarsus, but we had the same process. We were on the road to damnation and God spoke to us through the gospel. He stopped us in our hell-bent tracks.

Jesus said that no man could come to the Son unless the Father draws him. If you are a Christian, you were drawn to the Son by the Father. God even helps us in our repentance. (See 2 Timothy 2:25.) We are like Lazarus, so dead that we stink to high Heaven. (See John 11:39.) A proud person would never admit that. But by His grace, God calls our names and puts life into our dead bodies. Then it's up to us to come out of the tomb of this dark, evil world, and live in the light as a testimony to His amazing grace.

"Draw me, we will run after you" (Song of Solomon 1:4).

Hornet's Nest

We have decided to drop a cartoon of a hornet's nest now and then with some of my blogs. These seem to stir a buzz. Take, for instance, my saying that if someone had been in a good lightning storm and didn't come out of it fearing God, they were either blind or mentally challenged. That stirred some stinging responses. Atheists felt that I was saying that they were mentally challenged, when the truth is that they fit into the "blind" category, as we all once did. (See 2 Corinthians 4:1-2.) Another angry response flew at me from an atheist who spent some time saying that pigs were not unclean animals, and how they made great pets. Then he went into a delirious frenzy because the Bible said that people who go back to their sin were likened to pigs. Why was he so upset, when he believed that pigs were the best things since sliced bread?

"Therefore seeing we have this ministry, as we have received mercy, we faint not; but have renounced the hidden things of dishonesty, not walking in craftiness, nor handling the word of God deceitfully; but by manifestation of the truth commending ourselves to every man's conscience in the sight of God" (2 Corinthians 4:1-2).

ANOTHER WORD FOR ATHEISM IS DEFIANCE.

DEFIANCE

ATHEISM

TRUTH

Dinner With 40 Atheists

Late in 2007, a courageous Christian dropped a handful of one of our tracts ("The Atheist Test") at a gathering of atheists, who meet once a month at the local IHOP at the John Wayne Airport in Orange County, California. The atheists then invited me to join them for dinner on January 8, 2008. They requested that I get there an hour early to "set a baseline," because some of their members might get a bit hotheaded when discussing "religion." I accepted their invitation and decided to take my manager with me (Mark Spence, who is also the Dean of the School of Biblical Evangelism).

Before we went I got permission to also take a handheld HD camera. I was determined not to go there to win an argument, but to simply show that I deeply cared for them as people, since most atheists seem to have the impression that Christians don't like them. We arrived about five minutes early, shook hands, and sat down. After the orders were taken, I quietly approached the waiter and told him to give me the bill for the entire party.

When he brought it to me, I was almost shaking with excitement. If someone had tried to take it from me I would have physically fought him. (I felt like I used to feel with my kids early on Christmas morning.) When they found out that I had personally paid the tab, they were very grateful, polite, pleasant, kind, and extremely thankful. (See 1 Peter 2:15.) The experience was a highlight of my life.

Then about ten of us huddled around a table and talked about the things of God for about an hour. It was up close and personal. Mark answered every question and objection they had, calmly and eloquently. It's all on film and we hope to be able to make it available through the ministry soon for anyone who wants it. I took copies of my new book, *How to Know God Exists*, and all the folks at our table wanted one. It's a strange feeling when one is signing books for atheists. Then we posed for pictures and left, almost bursting with joy after such a wonderful opportunity to meet and talk with these dear people. Maybe the next time they meet for dinner, at the International House of *Prayer*, hundreds will show up saying, "We heard that this is the atheist group where you get a free meal." Seriously, though, please pray for the Orange County Atheists.

"For so is the will of God, that with well doing you may put to silence the ignorance of foolish men" (1 Peter 2:15).

DYING DOG

There is a temporary disadvantage for the Christian in that he or she is confined to always speaking the truth. In a sense, we have to fight with one hand tied behind our backs. However, there are no holds barred for those who don't fear God. Their weapons of warfare are lies, exaggerations, statements made out of context, hearsay, rabbit trails, misquotes, and false accusations. The unsaved fight against the claims of the gospel because they love their sin and disdain God's righteousness. They are a like a dying dog stuck in an ice-cold river, who viciously snaps at his rescuer. Let them bite ... we will still reach out while there is hope.

"The fruit of the righteous is a tree of life; and he that wins souls is wise" (Proverbs 11:30).

ATHEIST DICTATOR

We were filming the fourth season of our television program in Europe. It was the last day, after visiting thirteen countries in thirteen days, and we were preaching open air at a university in Romania. One of the students was an atheist who had been brought up in a Christian home and he was extremely vocal. He had broken the Ten Commandments, heard the good news of the gospel, but said that if God were real, He would stop him from leaving the crowd. Then he turned around and boldly walked back into the building to make his point. God didn't stop him from leaving. Did his actions prove anything? Yes, they proved that God doesn't take dictation from atheists. It doesn't work with presidents, either. If I say, "If the President of the United States exists, let him show up outside my house tonight!" I'm going to be standing alone in the dark. Such talk

is the epitome of arrogance. It was the arrogant Italian dictator Mussolini who stood on a pinnacle as a youth, and said that if God were real He should prove it by striking him dead. His prayer was eventually answered.

To say, "We told you hell was real!" will be no consolation for the faithful Christian. The stakes are too high for such shallow trifles.

"And immediately Jesus stretched forth his hand, and caught him, and said to him, O you of little faith, wherefore did you doubt?" (Matthew 14:31).

THE FOUR-LETTER WORD

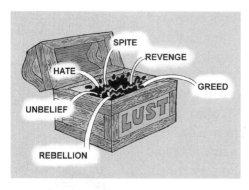

If you could sum up in one word what is stopping most people of this world from coming to Christ, what would that word be? Perhaps you would say unbelief, or rebellion, or sin. True, but I believe that it is lust that is at the forefront of sin. The Bible says that the corruption we see in the world has its roots in lust. (See 2 Peter 1:14.) Lust is the burning and shining light for Hollywood, soap operas, the Internet, magazine covers, TV programs, car advertising, the sale of clothes, popular music, and contemporary culture.

In 2 Peter 3:3 we are told that the reason why men mock God is because they love their lust. So, what would make any sane man turn from lust's powerful pleasure? Two reasons are apparent. The first is that we can never separate lust from death. If we embrace lust, we embrace death. A realization of that eternal truth should cause common sense to rise up in our human brains. No sane man wants to embrace death and with that, eternal damnation.

The second reason a man walks away from the pleasures of lust is the knowledge of what it cost the Savior to obtain his forgiveness. If my father sold everything he had to raise money to pay a fine for me to get out of prison, what sort of wretch would I be to go straight back into crime simply because I enjoyed it? The Prodigal Son made a sensible choice. The Bible says that he "came to himself." And that's the point to which we are trying to bring the lost. We want them to exercise common sense. All we are saying is, "Come to your senses and call on the name of the Lord. He will not only change your unclean desires, but He will also save you from death and hell."

When the power of the gospel changes a sinful and lust-loving heart, no amount of atheistic whining or evolutionary silliness comes close to making a Christian ever doubt the reality of God.

He who doesn't fear God has never been in a good lightning storm, is blind, or is severely mentally challenged.

"But every man is tempted, when he is drawn away of his own lust, and enticed" (James 1:14).

How to Have Your Cake

I was visiting an area of the country where it had snowed the previous night. The white blanket that covered the earth was as pure as the driven snow. The trees, bushes, houses, cars—everything—looked like a painted scene on a Christmas card. Snow is beautiful for about two days, and then it turns to sludge. Many marriages are the same. The heat comes on or the dirt comes in, and what was once pure and pristine bliss quickly becomes a horrible mess. So, how can you make your marriage work? To change the analogy, simply go by the recipe book, the Bible, use the ingredients suggested and your marriage will rise to your expectations. Of course, the world doesn't open the Bible because it knows better. The book either sits on a shelf gathering dust, or it's the object of prejudice and cynicism to the point where every word is mocked. But the ingredients are laid out for the Christian—selfless love, genuine kindness, quick forgiveness, self-control, true humility, and constant prayer.

Add the will of God, which is the most important factor in the relationship, and you can have your cake and eat it too.

"For the word of God is quick, and powerful, and sharper than any two-edged sword, piercing even to the dividing asunder of soul and spirit, and of the joints and marrow, and is a discerner of the thoughts and intents of the heart" (Hebrews 4:12).

Blood Is on Your Hands

"Only first trimester abortions are deemed within the woman's right to privacy," my critic informed me. "Second trimester is left up to the state to regulate, and third trimester may be outright outlawed. And to my knowledge, they are in every state. In other words, ain't nobody aborting babies that look like that."

You are gravely misinformed. Pictured is a twelve-week-old baby in the womb.

"I will praise you; for I am fearfully and wonderfully made.... My substance was not hid from you, when I was made in secret, and curiously wrought in the lowest

parts of the earth. Your eyes did see my substance, yet being imperfect; and in your book all my members were written, which in continuance were fashioned, when as yet there was none of them" (Psalm 139:14-16).

Questions and Objections

"I am learning so much about atheism," writes one seeker, "but it makes me wonder … Can you appeal to the conscience if it is seared?"

The answer is "Definitely." This is why. A seared conscience is not a dead conscience. In Scripture, the conscience is called "weak" (1 Corinthians 8:7-12), "good" (1 Timothy 1:5), "pure" (1 Timothy 3:9), "defiled" (Titus 1:15), and "evil" (Hebrews 10:22), but it's never called "dead."

In John 8:9, one would think that the accusing, self-righteous Pharisees would have had dead consciences, but we are told that when Jesus spoke of their sin, "… they which heard it, being convicted by their own conscience, went out one by one, beginning at the eldest, even to the last: and Jesus was left alone, and the woman standing in the midst." Not one of them escapes the accusatory voice of the conscience. It was Romans 2:15 in action: "… which show the work of the law written in their hearts, their conscience also bearing witness, and their thoughts the meanwhile accusing or else excusing one another."

However, I suspect that you are actually asking about casting our pearls before swine. When do we stop offering the gospel to the hardened unsaved? Perhaps a clue is given in the word "swine." The Scriptures use pigs to describe people who make a profession of faith, but go back to the world. (See 2 Peter 2:22.) It is an appropriate analogy, as the pig is considered to be an unclean animal. But the reason it wallows in filth is to cool its flesh. And that's the reason a false convert goes back to the filth of sin. His conversion is spurious and it's only a matter of time until he has to go back to the filth of the world to cool his flesh.

We often call these people backsliders, but they are, in reality, false converts, and most of us would agree that they are the hardest to reach with the true gospel. This is because they usually say that they were born again, read the Bible, went to church, witnessed, sang praise songs, etc., but then they saw the error of being a Christian. However, each of us needs to make the call as to whether or not to stop witnessing to such a person. If we do stop, that doesn't mean we give up on them. God forbid. We may stop sharing the gospel because they are contentious, but we should never stop praying for their salvation until the day death seizes them. Then, and only then, is the battle over.

"But it is happened to them according to the true proverb, The dog is turned to his own vomit again; and the sow that was washed to her wallowing in the mire" (2 Peter 2:22).

THE SECRET

Sometimes the world betrays itself and reveals its wicked heart. Take for example an interview with an actor who played a greedy oilman in a major motion picture. He said of the violent character he played, "What does a man, who has become an animal, do with himself? He emerges out of his burrow." The interviewer picked up on that and asked, "When you say when a man 'has become an animal,' I feel like that's just coming from within you."

He replied, "Yeah, yeah … there's something appealing about that, for sure."

More probing. "What's going through your mind in some of those scenes … where you kill a man?"

He answered, "It's a secret."

The interviewer asked, "Do you like to kill a man on camera? Do you enjoy those scenes?"

"Yes."

"Why?"

The actor replied, "I don't think I have a good answer for it."

He may not have a good answer for why he secretly loves to kill a man on camera, but the Bible does. Listen to Scripture describe the universal wickedness of the human heart:

"Their throat is an open sepulcher; with their tongues they have used deceit; the poison of asps is under their lips: Whose mouth is full of cursing and bitterness: Their feet are swift to shed blood: destruction and misery are in their ways: and the way of peace have they not known: There is no fear of God before their eyes" (Romans 3:13-18).

How true is the testimony of God's Word. We certainly do "love darkness and hate the light." However, the day will come when this actor's secret will be brought into the light. May he come to the Savior before that terrible day.

"For with you is the fountain of life: in your light shall we see light" (Psalm 36:9).

Now You Know

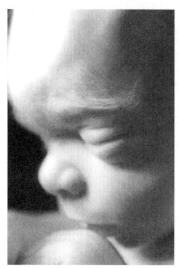

These are my words: "Pedophilia (molesting children), illegal. Abortion (killing children), legal." This is the response from a reader of my blog, who calls himself *Sinned34*: "Protecting children from predators is something most people can agree on. Preventing a collection of cells from being removed from a woman's body is not something most people can agree on."

My response: "This is a photo of a your 'collection of cells.' It's a five-month old baby in the womb. Now you can see what you are advocating killing. There's blood on your hands."

"You shall not kill" (Exodus 20:13).

Perfect Timing

Someone sent me a very cool Coca-Cola clock that lights up when it is plugged in. I hung it in the lobby of our ministry office, just above the cool Coca-Cola fridge that arrived anonymously a few weeks ago. So, I don't know who sent the cool fridge or the cool clock. Neither do I know if it's the same person that sent both, or two very kind people. So that means that I will have to continue to be nice to everyone. It may have even come from one of our

110

atheist friends. I did notice a loud ticking sound. (Calm down, Mr. Atheist. That was a joke. I know you would never think of such a thing.) Anyway, if it is one of you that did this, thank you. It is a wonderful blessing to me, and one that I see every day as I go to our ministry. I wonder if there's such a thing as a Coca-Cola Lamborghini?

> *"Rooted and built up in him, and stablished in the faith, as you have been taught, abounding therein with thanksgiving"* (Colossians 2:7).

HALF A YAWN

How do you feel when you are cultivating a sneeze and at the last second it dissipates? How about being interrupted when you are in the middle of a serious yawn? Have you ever had something that you were going to say, and at the last second it flies away from your mind like a bird into the distance? How do you feel when you forget a well-known actor's name? You can visualize his face, his name sits on the tip of your tongue, and after you run through the alphabet you conclude it's not in there.

Each of these experiences is frustrating. However, they are nothing compared to the ultimate frustration of being a thinking person, and looking for an explanation of life that you can never seem to find. Why are we here? What is life's purpose? Why am I waiting to die? Listen to this agonizing quote from Irish writer, dramatist, and poet, Samuel Beckett. He said, "Life is an indefinite waiting for an explanation that never comes." The terrible tragedy is that the explanation will never come, as long as the gospel is ignored.

"Who has saved us, and called us with an holy calling, not according to our works, but according to his own purpose and grace, which was given us in Christ Jesus before the world began" (2 Timothy 1:9).

Crazy Criminals

A criminal was condemned to die in the electric chair. The courts had appointed a lawyer on behalf of the criminal, and he had worked hard to get him a reprieve. Finally, it came through, signed by the governor himself. The excited lawyer delivered it by hand to the criminal, but he refused to look at it, and instead began insanely raving about his grandparents being monkeys and arguing about who made the prison in which he was incarcerated. Charles Spurgeon said, "All men are under the Law by nature, and consequently they are condemned by it because they have broken its commands; and apart from our Lord Jesus men are only reprieved criminals, respited from day to day, but still under sentence and waiting for the appointed hour when the warrant shall be solemnly executed upon them."

"But when the fullness of time was come, God sent forth his Son, made of a woman, made under the law, to redeem them that were under the law, that we might receive the adoption of sons" (Galatians 4:4-5).

> "SAVE SOME, O CHRISTIANS! BY ALL MEANS,
> SAVE SOME. FROM YONDER FLAMES AND OUTER
> DARKNESS, AND THE WEEPING, WAILING, AND
> GNASHING OF TEETH, SEEK TO SAVE SOME! LET
> THIS, AS IN THE CASE OF THE APOSTLE, BE YOUR
> GREAT, RULING OBJECT IN LIFE, THAT BY ALL
> MEANS YOU MIGHT SAVE SOME."
> CHARLES SPURGEON

From
Spurgeon Gold

INCONSISTENT LAWS

Pedophilia (molesting children), illegal. Abortion (killing children), legal. Fornication with a seventeen-year-old, illegal. Fornication with an eighteen-year-old, legal. The sale of pornography in public places, legal. The displaying of the Ten Commandments in public places, illegal.

"To the weak became I as weak, that I might gain the weak: I am made all things to all men, that I might by all means save some" (1 Corinthians 9:22).

QUESTIONS AND OBJECTIONS

An unbeliever writes, "Can you explain why the New Testament account of the Nativity contradicts itself when Herod the Great died in 4 BC and Cyrenius did not become Governor of Syria until 6 AD, leaving a ten-year gap between Matthew's and Luke's accounts? Also, any census (of which there is no record) would only have affected Roman citizens and there would have been no requirement for Mary and Joseph to travel to Bethlehem. Also, can you explain why you think that God is a loving deity when he orders Abraham to throw his

Herod the Great was king when Jesus was born but died very soon afterwards.
Matthew 2 and Luke 1

Herod Antipas was the son of Herod the Great. He had John beheaded. It was to this Herod that Jesus was brought for trial after His arrest
Matthew 14, Mark 6, Luke 3

Herod Agrippa, a grandson of Herod the Great. He persecuted the apostles and the Christians in Jerusalem.
Acts 4 27, 12:1-3, 13:1

own child on a bonfire and kill him? Okay, so he spares him at the last second, but think of how Isaac would have felt knowing that his father was prepared to kill him."

1. **Herod**: A little research is helpful with these sorts of difficulties, and there are plenty of them. Herod the Great (the first Herod) did die in 4 BC, but Herod Antipas is the one spoken of in the gospels. Different Herods. I'm sure skeptics of the future will question how George Bush could be the Governor of Texas, and President of the United States at the same time. Again, a little research helps.

2. **The Census**: There *is* a record. It's in the gospels.

3. **Abraham**: True, God told Abraham to offer his only son, and when he was about to kill him, God stopped him. It is important to understand that this incident is a picture of God actually *sacrificing* His only begotten Son to suffer on the Cross for our sins. Such is His love and mercy for rebels such as us.

"And you shall know the truth, and the truth shall make you free" (John 8:32).

Insulting Steel

In places where temperatures freeze, salt is routinely dropped on the roads to melt snow and make driving safer. However, such a practice also destroys cars. Salt, the same stuff we eat daily, eats steel daily. We are often reminded that

Jesus said of the Church "You are the salt of the Earth," and we are told that salt has many properties that remind us of what we are in Christ—preservation and flavor, to name just two.

But let us not forget that because God is with us, we are the most powerful force on Earth. No steel cage can stop a Christian from fulfilling the will of God. Jesus used an anthropomorphism to convey this fact when He spoke of the finger of God being with Him. That's all we need; a little divine backup. I have often said that a blind, anemic, weak-kneed flea on crutches has more chance of defeating a herd of ten thousand wild, stampeding elephants, than the enemy has of defeating God. So the next time he tries to intimidate you, think of the most powerful thunder and lightening storm you can, and remember that if God made that, and if He is with us, nothing can be against us.

"What shall we say then to these things? If God be for us, who can be against us?" (Romans 8:31).

Bible Inspiration

The Bible is amazing and it easily can be shown to any reasonable person that it is inspired by God. It was written over a period of around 1,600 years, by between forty and fifty authors from all walks of life, and yet there is a wonderful continuity of thought running throughout its pages. Take, for instance, the subject of righteousness, a word that is  used 291 times in the King James Version. Jesus died on the Cross because God demanded perfect justice to satisfy His perfect righteousness. Look now at the amazing continuity of Scripture: Psalm 9:8, warned that God "… shall judge the world in righteousness." The Book of Proverbs 11:4 warns again, "Riches profit not in the day of wrath: but righteousness delivers from death."

So, how can guilty sinners become righteous in the sight of a holy God? Hosea 10:12 tells us "… for it is time to seek the Lord, till he comes and rains righteousness upon you." It was on the Day of Pentecost that righteousness rained down from Heaven. Now God commands all men everywhere to repent. Why? "Because he has appointed a day in which He will judge the world in righteousness." (See Acts 17:31.) As the Apostle Paul was about to die, he said, "Henceforth there is laid up for me a crown of righteousness, which the Lord, the righteous judge, shall give me at that day: and not to me only, but to all them also that love his appearing" (2 Timothy 4:8).

In the meantime, you and I wait for a new Heaven and new Earth "… wherein dwells righteousness." (See 2 Peter 3:13.) So, what should we be doing as Christians while we wait? Daniel 12:3 tells us: "And they that be wise shall shine as the brightness of the firmament; and they that turn many to righteousness as the stars for ever and ever."

> *"All scripture is given by inspiration of God, and is profitable for doctrine, for reproof, for correction, for instruction in righteousness: that the man of God may be perfect, thoroughly furnished to all good works"* (2 Timothy 3:16-17).

THE COMMON DENOMINATOR

I enjoy reading biographies, but I have lost count of how many times I have read in them about the harmful influence of the modern gospel. I have waded through books where a husband professes faith in Jesus and yet beats his wife over and over. He apologizes, asks God for forgiveness, and then does it again. And again. The common denominator with all these professed converts is that they responded to a perverted gospel. They came to Jesus for a better, victorious, problem-free life.

In one book, the author gives his testimony, as a professing Christian: "I hadn't learned to accept God's love and grace … [I was] trying to win God's approval." These are symptoms of a false conversion. They reveal a shallow understanding, if not complete ignorance, of the purpose of the Cross. Before he professed faith in Jesus, someone said to him, "If you are willing to accept Christ, not only as Savior but also as Lord of your life—the leader, the quarterback—great things are possible."

That's a perversion of the gospel message. We are not to tell sinners that God's purpose is to give mankind happiness and fulfillment, and to allow him to get the best out of life. Nowhere in Scripture do we see that message being preached, yet it is the essence of the modern proclamation. It leaves the sinner ignorant of the fact that he is a criminal, and ignorant of the fact that God is his Judge. It is the recipe for a false conversion. I find that if I keep the analogy in the courtroom, as criminal and Judge, it keeps me from straying into the error of the modern gospel.

"The Lord shall judge the people" (Psalm 7:8).

WISE WORDS FROM RICHARD DAWKINS

Many who hear the evolution debate often hear scientific phrases, yet they are never told what these mean. So, in an effort to broaden our understanding of the issues, here is a short lesson for those who don't know the basics.

A "transitional form" is something that shows one form of life evolving, or changing, into another. Darwinian evolution, as proposed by Charles Darwin, said that mankind and primates (the monkey family) have a common ancestor. However, the contemporary theory of evolution teaches that man came directly from apes, and to back up the theory there are full-color graphics of bent apes growing taller over millions of years until they stand upright.

To be a little simplistic—there occurred what is called the "Big Bang," and from there water formed, primitive life appeared in the water, that life came up on land, became male and female primates, then evolved into modern man. In other words, mankind transitioned from one species into another. Apes became men and women. However, there is a big problem for those that believe this theory. They can't find the missing link between man and apes in the fossil record. The fossil record is the historical "record" of human and animal bones that lie beneath the soil or in the rocks.

A believer of the theory, who, when pressed to produce evidence of even one species-to-species transitional form in the fossil record, falls back on the predictable evolutionists' tactic of saying that he's not an expert. He says, "I am not a paleontologist, so take this ... with a grain of salt. I recommend that you contact a paleontologist who can explain to you what a transitional form actually is, and how many of them we actually have. I might remind you that the overwhelming consensus is that we have quite a few."

No, we don't have overwhelming evidence for transitional forms. Look at this quote from *Science Digest*: "The fossils that decorate our family tree are so scarce that there are still more scientists than specimens. The remarkable fact is that all the physical evidence we have for human evolution can still be placed, with room to spare, inside a single coffin."

That's not true either. They have no physical evidence for human evolution. None. After searching and studying quotes from paleontologists, I am convinced that those who spout evolution are guilty of paleontological quackery. Most of them would put Disney *imagineers* out of work. They have built a lucrative industry out of their imaginations that rivals televangelism. What's more, their wide-eyed supporters have the same simple-minded mentality that keeps money-hungry preachers in business.

For years I have listened to poker-faced evolutionists bluffing that they had a "few" transitional forms or enough for "inside a single coffin." But after doing research for *Evolution: A Fairy Tale for Grownups*, I know that they have nothing in their hands. They are bankrupt. There are no species-to-species transitional forms in the fossil record. None. The following quote is from Indiana University's website (brackets added): "According to the theory of evolution, the descent, with modification, road to humans (or any other group, for that matter) is paved with a sequence of transitional fossils . . . fortunately, some members of some of those groups were fossilized, and a few of those are found from time to time, giving us the hit-or-miss, very spotty record of fossils which has led us to hypothesize [imagine] that picture of a branched tree of being which we call evolution."

The problem is that the species-to-species transitional forms in the fossil record aren't "few," "hit or miss," or "very spotty." They don't exist. There aren't any, except in the imaginations of those who represent this pseudoscience called evolution. Here is another sincere believer providing me with "evidence": "The fact remains that at least evolution *has* physical evidence (and reams of it) to debate over.... Whether you're willing to accept the evidence we're able to produce in copious amounts is irrelevant in light of the fact that it does exist here and now and we can all see and argue over it. And there's not just one piece of evidence ... there's millions of years worth buried under our feet. The Cambrian Explosion period in prehistory that was found in British Columbia in the early 1900's has surely got to be enough to convince anyone. [Google it, if you're curious.] Read that book, *Wonderful Life* by Stephen Jay Gould, that I mentioned for all the evidence you could ever want, then you can visit any number of natural history museums to see it with your own eyes. What religious apologist could ever offer that kind of varied and immediate evidence? Happy hunting!"

All the Cambrian Explosion (a specific time in history) does is prove that creation came into being as though Someone suddenly created it. It disproves evolution: "And we find many of them [Cambrian fossils] already in an advanced state of evolution, the very first time they appear. It is as though they were just planted there, without any evolutionary history. Needless to say, this appearance of sudden planting has delighted creationists." (Richard Dawkins, *The Blind Watchmaker,* London: W.W. Norton & Company, 1987, p. 229.)

I asked for one piece of evidence of a species-to-species transitional form in the fossil record, and the best I was given was advice to visit museums and wished "happy hunting." Why should I have to do the hunting? All I want is one example. That will shut my mouth.

Charles Darwin said, "But, as by this theory innumerable transitional forms must have existed, why do we not find them embedded in countless numbers in the crust of the Earth? "

Well, have they found them? David M. Raup, Curator of Geology, Field Museum of Natural History, Chicago, said, " .. . we are now about 120 years after Darwin and the knowledge of the fossil record has been greatly expanded. We now have a quarter of a million fossil species, but the situation hasn't changed much."

Newsweek magazine said, "The more scientists have searched for the transitional forms between species, the more they have been frustrated." Evolutionist Stephen Jay Gould admitted, "The extreme rarity of transitional forms in the fossil record persists as the trade secret of paleontology." Lord Solly Zuckerman, MA, MD, DSc (Anatomy), added, "If man evolved from an apelike creature he did so without leaving a trace of that evolution in the fossil record."

Here are some more experts on the subject of evolution: "I would rather believe in fairy tales than in such wild speculation" (Nobel Prize winner Sir Ernst Chain). "Evolutionism is a fairy tale for grown-ups. This theory has helped nothing in the progress of science. It is useless" (Professor Louis Bounoure). "I have asked myself whether I may not have devoted my life to a fantasy" (Charles Darwin). "Darwinists are afraid. They are hiding something" (the actor Ben Stein). "Scientists who go about teaching that evolution is a fact of life are great con-men, and the story they are telling may be the greatest hoax ever" (Dr. T. N. Tahmisian—Atomic Energy Commission). "Ultimately, the Darwinian theory of evolution is no more nor less than the great cosmogenic myth of the twentieth century" (Michael J. Denton, Molecular Biologist). "I myself am convinced that the theory of evolution, especially the extent to which it's been applied, will be one of the great jokes in the history books of the future. Posterity will marvel that so very flimsy and dubious an hypothesis could be accepted with the incredible credulity that it has" (Malcolm Muggeridge, journalist and philosopher, Pascal Lectures, University of Waterloo Research *The Advocate*, March 8, 1984, p. 17).

Again, there is no extreme rarity of species-to-species transitional forms. They simply don't exist. I think that believers in the theory of evolution should take notice of the wise words of well-known evolutionist, Richard Dawkins: "And, next time somebody tells you that something is true, why not say to them: 'What kind of evidence is there for that?' And if they can't give you a good answer, I hope you'll think very carefully before you believe a word they say."

(From *Evolution: A Fairy Tale for Grownups*, published by Bridge-Logos, 2008.)

"Lead me in your truth, and teach me: for you are the God of my salvation; on you do I wait all the day" (Psalm 25:5).

WHAT MADE ALBERT REALLY ANGRY

"Skippy" quotes me as saying, "Talk about opposites, the awesome brilliance and creativity of Almighty God and the utter stupidity and dullness of an atheist." Then he says, "It'd be rather smarmy of me to criticize your spelling where you're calling other people stupid, but stupidity and dullness you say? Stupid like, say, Albert Einstein, Stephen Hawking, Thomas Edison, and Carl Sagan?"

Stephen Hawking

Skippy, I think that you are implying that both Albert Einstein and Stephen Hawking (two of the greatest minds in history) were atheists. Please read the following quotes slowly:

"In view of such harmony in the cosmos which I, with my limited human mind, am able to recognize, there are yet people who say there is

no God. But what really makes me angry is that they quote me for the support of such views" (Albert Einstein).

He's talking about *you*, Skippy.

"It would be very difficult to explain why the universe should have begun in just this way, except as the act of a God who intended to create beings like us" (Stephen Hawking, author of *A Brief History of Time*). These quotes are from *Evolution: A Fairy Tale for Grownups*.

"The heavens declare the glory of God; and the firmament shows his handiwork" (Psalm 19:1).

THROWING DOWN THE GAUNTLET

"Oh, wow, Ray," says my evolutionist friend Joel, "I'm flattered that you think I'm ripping this stuff off from someone smarter or more knowledgeable than I am."

I have to be honest with you, Joel, evolutionists are not smart. The theory is an intellectual embarrassment. It has nothing to do with true science. Prove me wrong. Give me one undeniable example of a transitional form in the fossil record that clearly shows one species evolving into another. Just one example. You can't do it. Don't tell me that museums are full of them, because they aren't. They don't have one. Don't cut and paste from Berkeley University's site—their examples are a joke. Big words and long names, bone fragments and glued feathers on fish won't do. Neither will any silliness about bacteria—that is not species-to-species evolution. There is no evidence of any species- to-species transitional form in the fossil record. None. Zilch. Okay? I'm waiting.

"In the beginning God created the heaven and the earth" (Genesis 1:1).

CHEATED ATHEISTS

I love thunder and lightning, especially when a boom is so loud that it makes the house shudder. I love to see massive lightning flashes across the sky when they make a pitch-dark night as bright as noonday. I love it because it puts the fear of God into me, and the fear of God is good for any human being. The atheist has convinced himself that God didn't create creation. For him creation doesn't exist, because if he calls it "creation," logic demands a Creator. We are instead surrounded by accidentation (yes, Mr. Atheist, I just made up another word, especially for you). Everything is a big accident. No one caused it and no one is in control.

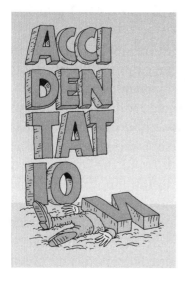

So when the atheist hears a boom of thunder, or sees an incredible flash of lightning, the thunder doesn't awaken him and the lightning doesn't give him light as to what is going on. He, because of what is called willful ignorance, cheats himself of perhaps the greatest of all benefits in this life—the fear of the Lord, which is "the beginning of wisdom." Without having the beginning of wisdom, he will keep thinking that nothing created everything, from nothing. Such thoughts only make sense to someone who hasn't got sense.

"The fear of the Lord is the beginning of wisdom" (Psalm 111:10).

Daredevils

Every sane person develops a healthy fear of danger as they mature in life. As children, we learn that fire is hot and falling from heights can be painful. These are self-preserving fears. But there are some adults, called daredevils, who ignore those fears and instead try to cheat death. They are perhaps called dare*devils* because the devil is the one that once had power over death. (See Hebrews 2:14-15.) He,  as the chief executioner, had the legal right to take the lives of every human being because we are law-breakers under the sentence of death. (See Romans 6:23.)

That legal power was taken from him when Jesus paid our fine with His life's blood, and rose from the grave. (See Revelation 1:18.) Through repentance and faith in the Savior, the Christian has his death sentence commuted. Our case is dismissed because the evidence of our transgressions is washed away. The Judge of the Earth, in His great mercy, legally allows us to live. No wonder the Bible calls what we have in Christ the "unspeakable gift." No words can express what good news this is for dying humanity, that everlasting life is the gift of God! So, be a *you-know-what* and ignore the fear that seeks to stop you from sharing this good news with those who are still ignorant as to what actually happened on that Cross so long ago.

"Thanks be to God for his unspeakable gift" (2 Corinthians 9:15).

SURVIVAL OF THE FATTEST

Experts are now saying that obesity will kill more people than all cancers combined. An amazing ninety-seven-million Americans are overweight. Perhaps a bit self-control-challenged? Hundreds of thousands in the U.S. will die this year because they are obese or are on their way there. A study of over a quarter of a million U.S. children found that nearly one in five between seven and thirteen years of age was classified as overweight. That means, "By the year 2040, for the first time ever in our species, our life expectancy is expected to drop." Experts are becoming very concerned.

I cannot figure evolutionists out. Why the worry? Evolution will make sure that the species of fat kids will have fat kids, who will have fat kids, and each of them will evolve fatter veins to carry more fat through the blood to a fatter heart. It will make sure that they will have fat-tolerant livers, fat-tolerant colons, and fat-tolerant gall bladders, much larger knees to take the greater weight, and it will all be worked out by the much-evolved and chubby brain in our fat heads. So, a quiet word to those of the species who are becoming worried that we are not going to survive. Keep believing. Evolution has taken millions of years to bring Homo sapiens this far, and it will make sure that everything will get sorted out, in time.

"And he said, Take heed that you be not deceived" (Luke 21:8).

UNTYING KNOTS

Many an uneducated cyberspace atheist can create a painting of himself as an intellectual by some quick cutting and pasting. Certain words, e.g., Zeus, Thor, and other big words here and there, reveal that the painting is a copy. Other clues are objections about biblical civil laws such as the stoning of children for disobedience. Through atheist websites, the potential doubter can be given just enough rope from the Bible to hang himself. At these sites they will find out-of-context verses, illogical explanations, and untrue and ignorant claims. But, as a Christian, you are told to redeem the time because the days are evil, so you can save yourself time by joining the cut-and-paste club. Address their questions, but don't deny your family their time or don't spend hours trying to reason with someone who is proud of heart. You have better things to do. All you need to do is go to www.evidencebible.com and cut and paste from one hundred of the most common, and predictable questions asked by skeptics. The specific address is www.evidencebible.com/witnessingtool/browse.shtml.

There you will find out how these folks twist a Scripture to try and justify their love for sin. For every knot they tie, now you don't have to spend ages untying them. For example, an atheist says that his morality is based on the issue of happiness. That could take you some time to unravel. He says that if an action or thought hurts someone, then it is evil. That's the basis for godless morality. If it doesn't hurt anyone, then it's morally good. Answer that by saying, "So atheists say that child pornography is morally okay, as long as the pictures are taken without the children's knowledge. It doesn't hurt them, and it makes a lot of perverts happy." Good

and evil has nothing to do with the happiness of man. Sin is transgression of God's Law. When we sin, we sin against Him and Him alone. Anything else in comparison is peripheral.

"Against you, you only, have I sinned, and done this evil in your sight" (Psalm 51:4).

THE ELEGANCE OF SCIENCE

"Without logic," my friend Joel writes, "science would not exist. We can both agree with that, can't we? The elegance of science is that all its discoveries reinforce the rest. If something does not fit in, no matter how much we might want it to and no matter how long we have accepted it as true, it is rejected and a better answer is sought. This is the reason that something like the Big Bang Theory is on the outs in the scientific community."

Joel, here are some questions for you. If science couldn't exist without logic, where then did logic come from? Is it eternal? Did it have a beginning? Be careful that you are not adamant in your reply, because of your elegance of science statement. When science rejects its convictions for a better answer, it is an admission that science is continually finding that what it once believed is now wrong. How could you think that that is good? One minute science believes the Big Bang Theory, and then it doesn't. That means that what you are so adamantly arguing for as absolute truth at the moment could change in the next. And you are okay with that. That's illogical. Admit it Joel—you are like the rest of us. You love your sins, and all this mumbo-jumbo is just a cover up. Your Watergate isn't watertight.

WHERE DID THAT LATEST SCIENTIFIC THEORY GET TO!?!

I would be grateful if you would read John 3:19-21, and give me your thoughts.

> *"For men shall be lovers of their own selves, covetous, boasters, proud, blasphemers, disobedient to parents, unthankful, unholy, without natural affection, trucebreakers, false accusers, incontinent, fierce, despisers of those that are good, traitors, heady, high-minded, lovers of pleasures more than lovers of God"* (2 Timothy 3:2-4).

How to Beat a Hangover

If you are going to drink alcohol, here is some information about how to treat hangovers from an expert. He maintains that one of the causes of a hangover is dehydration, so he suggests that you drink plenty of fluids when you drink alcohol, such as water, fruit juices, or sodas. Then, the next morning when it hits you like an eighteen-wheeler, drink plenty of fluids, such as water, fruit juices, or sodas. He says that the symptoms you will get from a hangover are headache, muscle aches, fatigue, decreased attentiveness, lack of concentration, difficulty sleeping, dry mouth, nausea, vomiting, and diarrhea. Besides drinking liquids, he suggests not staying in bed all day, and then in just eight- to twenty-four hours you will feel a lot better. Those are his thoughts. Here's a suggestion from someone who isn't an expert on the best way to beat a hangover. Have the good sense not to drink alcohol. Duh.

> *"Wine is a mocker, strong drink is raging: and whosoever is deceived thereby is not wise"* (Proverbs 20:1).

HIDING BEHIND ANONYMITY

Nameless said, "So you're pro-life. You think that you're doing the right thing? No, all you're doing is taking rights away from pregnant women. But why would you care, it's not like you could ever get pregnant, so it doesn't concern you either way. No one is making anyone get an abortion, so shut up and let women have the right to get an abortion!"

Dear Nameless, (but you're not nameless to God—He knows your name, every hair on your head, and every thought of your desperately wicked heart.) Of course I'm pro-life. The word *murderer* and the word *Christian* cannot go together. Of course, the words murderer and religion go hand in hand. They have done so through history. No argument there. So make sure the two words don't confuse you. They are as different as night and day.

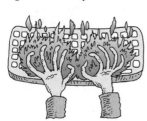

Nameless said, "Hey, before you start talking about atheists, why don't you get to know them? It seems to me that you don't have a clue about what atheists are really like. Why don't you talk with some atheists, and then come up with an opinion before you talk about them. I mean, after all, religious people have a far bigger problem with atheists than atheists have with religious people. And if you want to prove me wrong, then print my comment, unless of course you only want to show the comments of the people that agree with you. So prove me wrong, Ray, if you aren't afraid of people disagreeing with you."

"You shall not kill" (Exodus 20:13).

HEY, MR. ATHEIST

I have a couple of questions for you. What is it that you trust in to give you peace and joy? What gives you your sense of security for the future? Let me see if I can guess where your faith is directed. Is it toward money? Do you love it? Come on, admit it. Does having money in the bank give you a sense of peace and security? Is it your source of joy? Of course it is. Listen to what Jesus said about your attitude to money (mammon) and to God: "No one can serve two masters; for either he will hate the one and love the other, or else he will be loyal to the one and despise the other. You cannot serve God and mammon" (Matthew 6:24). Mr. Atheist, He's right isn't He? You can't fault the words of Jesus. I dare you to try and find something that He said that was erroneous. Bet you can't.

"For the love of money is the root of all evil: which while some coveted after, they have erred from the faith, and pierced themselves through with many sorrows" (1 Timothy 6:10).

PLANE SPEAKING

The difference between a Christian and an atheist is that the atheist waits until turbulence hits before he prays.

"Pray without ceasing" (1 Thessalonians 5:17).

Bad News for Zoos

No doubt not too many people will be excited about taking their families to the zoo, after a four-year-old tiger killed a man and mauled two others at the San Francisco Zoo, in late December of 2007. How frightening it would be to be chased by a big cat, whose sole intent is to rip your body to pieces and then eat it. Around the time of the attack I spotted a bumper sticker on an atheist web site that said, "Too many Christians. Not enough lions." Nice folks. One comment on the site said that it was a clever bumper sticker.

Actually, no one can kill a Christian. It has been well said that death isn't the termination of existence, but the entrance into an eternal and unchanging state. The Christian has been sealed with the life of God. All a murderer does is promote those who trust in Christ from this pain-filled, futile existence, into reality. Then, in the coming Kingdom we will enjoy forever an Earth where the lion will lie down with the lamb.

"For me to live is Christ, and to die is gain" (Philippians 1:21).

What Word?

A proud man picked the emergency instructions out of the seat pocket, as he sat in a plane that was about to crash. He laughed cynically at the graphics on the cover, and said that he could have done better. As he glanced at the text, he noticed what be believed to be a spelling mistake on the front page. The mistake was his, but because of his belief, he didn't even bother to open its pages. Instead, he mumbled something about the airline using scare tactics, ripped up the instructions, and for some reason became angry with the other passengers and tried to stop them from reading them. What word would you use to describe such a person?

"The foolishness of man perverts his way" (Proverbs 19:3).

Bowing Down to Anything

"I've always wondered," writes Joel, "what the effigy of Christ on the Cross that's found in most churches is, if not an idol? In days of yore, I can specifically remember praying to that effigy and seeing many others pray to it. I'm confused as to how that doesn't count as worshiping a graven idol, as is clearly forbidden in the Ten Commandments. Is it simply considered to be a relay station for prayers on their way to God and thus sanctified through a holy loophole?"

Joel, that's a good question. I don't know if you're an atheist because many people who are now high profile atheists are ex-Catholics. (See my book, Hollywood Be Thy Name for details.) The second of the Ten Commandments forbids paying homage, bowing down, to any graven image of any likeness, anywhere. The Roman Catholic Church got around it by removing the Second Commandment and splitting the last one into two

Commandments, to make up the ten. It sounds hard to believe, so check it out for yourself on the Vatican web site: (www.vatican.va/archive/ccc_css/archive/catechism/command.htm).

Here's the Second Commandment from the Bible: "You shall not make for yourself a graven image, or any likeness of anything that is in heaven above, or that is in the earth beneath, or that is in the water under the earth; you shall not bow down to them or serve them ..." (Exodus 20:4). Here is the Tenth Commandment: "You shall not covet your neighbor's house; you shall not covet your neighbor's wife, or his manservant, or his maidservant, or his ox, or his ass, or anything that is your neighbor's" (Exodus 20:17). The Roman Catholic Catechism, the official teaching of the church, removes the Second Commandment completely and splits the Ninth Commandment so that the second won't be missed. Here's how they split it, and I have copied the following directly from the site: "9. You shall not covet your neighbor's wife. 10. You shall not covet your neighbor's goods." I hope this helps.

"Who changed the truth of God into a lie, and worshipped and served the creature more than the Creator, who is blessed forever. Amen" (Romans 1:25).

"ATHEISM IS A CRUTCH FOR THOSE WHO CANNOT BEAR THE REALITY OF GOD."
TOM STOPPARD

Eternal Salivation

Someone once said, "Everything I love in life is illegal, immoral, or fattening." That's the testimony of many of us, until we come to the Cross. A new heart helps us deal with wanting to drive over the speed limit, or do anything that is immoral. However, I have to admit, I still have a love for things that are fattening, and I don't think I'm alone. How about popcorn and pecans covered in caramel? What about steaming hot chocolate pudding with a mountain of ice cream on top, then whipped cream on top of that, and to top it off, a cherry on the top? Huh? What about a pile of chocolate-covered macadamia nuts? Do you see a pattern here? I could go on about pastries and pies, cake and cookies, but I will spare you.

So, why is it that so many of life's wonderfully delicious pleasures for which we have such an appreciation, have negative repercussions? Perhaps it's just another part of living in a fallen creation. Picnics have flies, ants, and mosquitoes. Dreams have nightmares. Babies have colic, seas have sharks, roses have thorns, life has death, and chocolate has calories. Not long to go: "Eye has not seen, nor ear heard, nor have entered into the heart of man the things which God has prepared for those who love Him" (1 Corinthians 2:9). Eternal salivation, indeed!

"And this is the record, that God has given to us eternal life, and this life is in his Son" (1 John 5:11).

Fear or Trembling?

An inquirer asks, "Would you please elaborate on the concept of fear in this context: when you speak of fear, do you mean respect and reverence or terror?"

I can't separate the two. Jesus said, "And fear not them which kill the body, but are not able to kill the soul: but rather fear him which is able to destroy both soul and body in hell" (Matthew 10:28). Obviously, we are to reverence God. But that verse is speaking of far more than reverence. It is a trembling at the thought of what God can do to us. This concept of God is contrary to the popular "God is our buddy" type of contemporary Christianity. He can cast our body and soul into hell. That is truly terrifying. Look now at the Psalmist as he says the same thing: "My flesh trembles for fear of you; and I am afraid of your judgments" (Psalm 119:120). Why did he tremble? Because he was afraid of God's judgments.

When the Bible spoke of the coming of Jesus as a babe, we are told, "He shall save His people from their sins." Why didn't the angel say that He would save us from hell? Because it is sin that will take us to hell. It is the crime that sends the criminal to prison. If you want to keep a criminal out of prison, keep him out of crime. If I am saved from sin, I am saved from hell, and it is a healthy fear of God that keeps me away from the pleasures of alluring sins. When sin flutters its seductive eyes, I see only the fear of God, and turn away. It is that fear that keeps me trusting in Christ minute by minute and will keep me out of hell.

If I were introduced to the President of the United States, I would have a reverential fear because of his office, his political position. However, I wouldn't be afraid of him harming me. Does that mean that as a Christian I live in a state of constant paranoia? Of course not. It actually means I live in a constant sense of love and security. It's the same kind of fear that a child has for his loving father. Why doesn't the child run with the local gang of kids and create havoc in his neighborhood? Because he knows that if he did, he would be heading for a good whoopin' in the woodshed. The child knows that his dad loves him enough to set boundaries, and even at his young age he knows that those boundaries were set for his good. No other reason.

> *"The fear of the Lord is the beginning of knowledge: but fools despise wisdom and instruction"* (Proverbs 1:7).

Tough Time Financially?

If you are feeling the pinch, I have an idea that might help you get on your feet. I'm not necessarily thinking of greedy atheists that contact me, but rather families that are struggling. But if a greedy atheist runs with this, that's okay.

Here's my idea. Go door to door and offer to pay cash for the unused toys that most parents and grandparents have in their attics or basements, toys that kids and grandkids have outgrown. I would gladly get rid of a pile of unused toys for twenty-five dollars. Just buy ones that can be easily washed with those high-powered hoses. Get an empty store, put up a sign that says "Toy Swap," and allow customers to bring in their unused toys and swap them for the ones their kids like. Charge a fee to swap each one—one dollar for real small toys, three dollars for average size, and five dollars for larger plastic bikes, etc. I think it would take off.

Toys 'R Us would probably pay you to stay out of business. Then again, it may stimulate the toy industry. Whatever the case, I wish you well.

"Keep therefore the words of this covenant, and do them, that you may prosper in all that you do" (Deuteronomy 29:9).

"IT AMAZES ME TO FIND AN INTELLIGENT PERSON WHO FIGHTS AGAINST SOMETHING WHICH HE DOES NOT AT ALL BELIEVE EXISTS."
— GANDHI

ATHEIST MISSIONS

There are tens of thousands of Christian missions around the world that feed the homeless and take care of the poor. So I thought I would see how many atheist missions came up on the Internet. I typed in "Atheist Missions," and guess how many came up? Zip. I tried the search words "atheists feed the poor." None. "Atheists helping the homeless." No results. I got more results from typing in "hen's teeth."

So, Mr. Atheist, if the economy turns sour and leaves you homeless, thank God that there are Christian missions out there that will feed you, clothe you, and give you and your children somewhere to sleep. If you find yourself in a disaster, thank God for the Salvation Army, which is Christian-based, or the Red Cross, also Christian-based. Or if you are taken to a hospital because of a serious illness, you may end up in a Saint John's, a Saint Jude's, or some other hospital whose name reminds us of its roots.

One more thought. If you find yourself in a lifeboat with no food and a group of very hungry people who are checking you out as their lunch (it has happened), who would you rather be sharing the lifeboat with—a group of starving evolutionists who believe in survival of the fittest and have no moral absolutes, or with a group of Christians, who love their neighbor as themselves and fear God?

> *"And if it seem evil to you to serve the Lord, choose this day whom you will serve, whether the gods which your fathers served that were on the other side of the flood, or the gods of the Amorites, in whose land you dwell; but as for me and my house, we will serve the Lord"* (Joshua 24:15).

WHERE'S MOSES?

The Scriptures tell us that the Israelites lost sight of Moses when he was on Mt. Sinai. They asked Aaron to make them their own god. So Aaron, listening to the voice of the people, asked the Israelites to contribute from their possessions to make an idol, and everyone had something to give. He then created the golden calf, and that's what Israel bowed down to. (See Exodus 32.)

When church leaders listen to the voice of the people, they end up with an idol. If we asked America what their image of God is like, most would give their contribution and say that He is loving, kind, merciful, and good. "God is a good God"

isn't just alliteration. It is the image America has of God, and it has created that image because it has lost sight of Moses.

When the Law is preached, suddenly God isn't only good, but He is perfect, holy, just, and good. Without the Law of Moses to give us perspective on the character of God, we end up worshiping a golden calf, and when mammon is worshiped, like Israel, the nation ends up in a sexual orgy. And then comes the predictable judgment of God. The only way to bring this nation to its senses is to do what Moses did—cast the Law down at its feet, show them that they have broken it into a thousand pieces, and ask, "Who is on the Lord's side?"

"For Moses had said, Consecrate yourselves today to the Lord, even every man upon his son, and upon his brother; that he may bestow upon you a blessing this day" (Exodus 32:29).

Rammed Down the Throat

In 1982, a Gallup Poll asked Americans if they believed that God created mankind. An amazing 82 percent said that they believed He did. In 2007, the same question was asked, and 81 percent said they thought that God created man. So, despite evolution being rammed down the throats of school children and television viewers for more than fifty years, the belief in

intelligent design dropped only one percent. It seems that the average person isn't easily fooled by all the lies. www.gallup.com/poll/21814/Evolution-Creationism-Intelligent-Design.aspx

"Let them praise the name of the Lord: for he commanded, and they were created" (Psalm 148:5).

Worse Than His Bite

I noticed that one of the atheists who communicates with me said that he knows all about the Bible because he was once a "strong Christian." Hold it there for a moment. He was once a strong Christian? Let's analyze what he is saying. A Christian is someone who knows the Lord: "And this is eternal life, that they may know You, the only true God, and Jesus Christ whom You have sent" (John 17:3; see also Hebrews 8:11).

So our atheist friend is admitting that he knew the Lord? Or is he admitting that God is real and he has turned his back on Him? If confronted with such a thought, he will predictably say, "I thought I knew the Lord." If that's the case, then he was never a Christian. He thought he was, but he wasn't. He was a false convert.

One well-known atheist who has "an itinerant ministry" says that he was a Christian pastor for seventeen years. That's impressive. Judas only managed to fake it for three-and-a-half years. This man faked it for seventeen years, and in a pulpit! His name is Dan Barker. A number of years ago I emailed Dan and explained about the Judas thing. Barker bit back that if I ever contacted him again, I would hear from his service providers. Wow! I must have struck a *roar* nerve (deliberate misspelling).

We often call these people bitter backsliders. However, they aren't backsliders, because they never slid forward in the first place. The correct term for them is false converts. They are mentioned in Mark 4 and in the writings of Peter, where they are likened to a pig that goes back to its filth, and a dog that returns to its vomit.

"The sower sows the word. And these are they by the way side, where the word is sown; but when they

141

have heard, Satan comes immediately, and takes away the word that was sown in their hearts" (Mark 4:14-15).

His Name Was Mudd

Have you ever heard of Dr. Samuel Mudd? He was the doctor who treated the broken leg that John Wilkes Booth sustained when he jumped from the balcony at Ford's Theater after assassinating Abraham Lincoln. Dr. Mudd was found guilty of conspiracy by a military court in the death of President Lincoln. He escaped being hanged by one vote, and was delivered to a mosquito-infested prison off the coast of Florida, called Dry Tortugas, that was said to be a hell on Earth.

When Hollywood made a movie of the life of Dr. Mudd, they wrote across the doorway of the prison: "Leave hope behind, all who enter here." What a terrible thought—that any human being would have to enter a place that has no hope. The world describes hopelessness by saying, "He hasn't a hope in hell." What fearful truths the world often says in passing.

There will be no hope of escape for those who are damned in hell forever. The Bible asks a rhetorical question, "How shall we escape if we neglect so great salvation" (Hebrews 2:3). How we must pray with earnest passion, be true and faithful in our witness, and plead with this dying world with the utmost sobriety.

"For the grave cannot praise you, death cannot celebrate you: they that go down into the pit cannot hope for your truth" (Isaiah 38:18).

ATHEIST PARANOIA

Joshua S. Black, when addressing an atheist, said, "For people who don't believe in God, you guys sure are paranoid about something!" How true that is. I have known many atheists, and I have found them to be totally committed to their negative cause. They are zealots, fanatics who are serious, angry, hateful, and blasphemous toward something they don't believe in. And what's more, they spend their time gathering fuel for the fire of their hatred against God and those who love Him. They gather what they think is legitimate fuel, whether it is atrocities committed by the hypocritical religions of history, or the horrors of the Inquisition.

They even gather unintelligent and unscientific material. It qualifies for use because it fits their presuppositions. Any fuel will do, as long at it puts smoke between them and the God they hate. It was Jonathon Miller who said, "In some awful, strange, paradoxical way, atheists tend to take religion more seriously than the practitioners." So, what is this "something" about which they are so paranoid? It is the same "something" that makes criminals paranoid, and it is that paranoia that fuels criminals to have a deep-rooted hatred for the police. It is not the individual officer they hate; it's what he stands for—civil law. And that's the root of the hatred that the atheist has for God and for those who represent Him.

Once again, the Bible has said this all along. It hits the nail on its big, hard head: "… because the mind of the flesh [with its carnal thoughts and purposes] is hostile to God, for it does not submit itself to God's Law; indeed it cannot" (Romans 8:7, The Amplified Bible). They hate

the morality that God's Law demands. That is the fuel for their hostility.

"For to be carnally minded is death; but to be spiritually minded is life and peace" (Romans 8:6).

The Mother of Knowledge

I had an uncle who repeated almost everything my aunt said. It wasn't a full repetition; it was rather the last five or six words of her sentences. The repeating began while she was still finishing her thoughts. He probably didn't even know he was doing it. He was simply echoing what was being said. Once I noticed it, I was fascinated by it and, as a child, it sure helped me remember what she said.

It's been observed that repetition is the mother of knowledge. Repetition is the mother of knowledge. If you want to get God's Word into your memory, write it down, then review it, and review it again. Then repeat it out loud, again, and then again, until it automatically echoes in your mind. Three times, in a matter of a couple of minutes, Jesus repeated the necessity of the new birth as a means of entering Heaven. (See John 3:1-7.) Three times.

Never be slow to repeat this truth in the ears of the unsaved. They need to hear it again and again until it sinks into their minds—we have angered God and we are heading for hell. No amount of good works can save us, only the grace of God in Jesus Christ, through the new birth. Those who surrender to the Savior usually say that they had heard the gospel repeated many times, but suddenly it was the first time they actually "heard" it.

"So then faith comes by hearing, and hearing by the word of God" (Romans 10:17).

Within the Sound of the Pulpit

I have deep sadness when I listen to many of America's popular preachers. They have stripped the gospel of that which is designed to awaken its hearers, and replaced it with a message of life-enhancement. And I suspect that they have no idea what they have done. Their large congregations and commendations from the world have confirmed them in their error.

They are like a doctor who became extremely popular because he never used a needle to inoculate his ever-increasing number of patients against a deadly disease. He didn't like the feeling he got when the needle gave them pain, so his discarded it in the name of love. When his patients began to die of an agonizing disease, his professed love was seen for what it was—a terrible betrayal.

Millions of unconverted churchgoers sit in pews with Bibles on their laps, asleep in their sins, within earshot of the pulpit. Listen to these sobering words of warning from J. C. Ryle: "It is a fearful thing to fall into the hands of the living God, but never so fearful as when men fall from under the gospel. The saddest road to hell is that which runs under the pulpit, past the Bible, and through the midst of warnings and invitations." How much sadder is it when there is no warning given.

"How then shall they call on him in whom they have not believed? And how shall they believe in him of whom they have not heard? And how shall they hear without a preacher?" (Romans 10:14).

145

Bitter Man

A college teacher in Red Oak, Iowa, maintained that he was fired after telling his students not to interpret the story of Adam and Eve as being literal. Steve Bitterman, sixty, who was teaching a western civilization course said he often used excerpts from the Old Testament as part of the class. Bitterman said: "I'm just a little bit shocked myself that a college in good standing would back up students who insist that people who have been through college and have a master's degree, a couple actually, have to teach that there were such things as talking snakes or lose their job."

So, Bitterman doesn't believe in talking snakes. I wonder if he believes in talking parrots, or primates that communicate in sign language, or dolphins that converse with each other? However, he has master's degrees, so he more than likely knows that animals are too dumb to actually talk. They are not as intelligent as modern man, who thinks that he came from a bang that came from nothing, that became a fish which over millions of years discarded its gills, evolved lungs, grew arms and legs, crawled up out of the ocean, tossed away its fins, became male and female, and then learned to talk.

"Professing themselves to be wise, they became fools" (Romans 1:22).

THIS IS JUST FOR MEN

Someone once asked me the question, "What's the difference between in-laws and outlaws?" The answer was that outlaws are wanted. I am fortunate, because I have wonderful in-laws who love the Lord. Some people don't, and it's a scary fact of life that a man doesn't just marry a wife, he marries her whole family. He may, therefore, have a lifetime of rubbing shoulders with people he doesn't like. The unwanted in-laws problem can put a strain on any marriage, but as Christians, the love of God in us can help solve the problem. Jesus said to love our enemies.

A lack of finances can be another strain. A big one. So don't let covetousness and credit cards pull you into debt. Contentment is born out of thanksgiving; contentment is the enemy of greed. If a burglar tries to break into your house, you wouldn't send your wife to the door. As a man, you could never do that. So, don't send your wife to the door spiritually. Take the lead. Don't let the thief who came to kill, steal, and destroy, steal time with your wife and destroy your marriage. You initiate prayer together. You read the Scriptures with her daily.

And here's something else that will help your marriage. It's a principle that took me years to learn. When your wife has a problem she's dealing with, just let her talk it out. Don't offer solutions. I know it's hard, but believe it or not, she doesn't want a solution. She just wants a listening ear. I know it sounds strange, but we are talking about a different species here. Do you like messing around in a women's

shoe store for hours? Nope. She does. Do you like talking while the TV is on? Nope. She does. Do you give every tiny detail about a newborn baby? Nope. She does. They are a different species. So deal with it and just listen. It works. For further instruction about men and women, see *101 Things That Husbands Do to Annoy Their Wives*. My wife, Sue, helped me write it in ten minutes.

"And be kind one to another, tender-hearted, forgiving one another, even as God for Christ's sake has forgiven you" (Ephesians 4:32).

"Ye are the light of the world. A city that is set on an hill cannot be hid" (Matthew 5:14).

WHY BOTHER?

Atheists are guilty of what they often accuse Christians of doing—using circular reasoning. They say embarrassingly unintelligent things, such as: "You can't prove the flying spaghetti monster doesn't exist, and I can't prove that God doesn't exist. You therefore have an obligation to prove that God exists." No we don't. The burden of proof doesn't lie with the Christian.

If someone is so irrational as to say that my car had no maker, I am under no obligation to try to prove to him that it does. The man is obviously mentally deranged, and the Bible says, "Answer not a fool according to his folly" (Proverbs 26:4). So why do we bother answering at all? Because the next verse in Proverbs has a special dispensation for a certain type of fool. If he is "wise in his own conceit," if he thinks his foolish argument is clever (how well that describes the average atheist), then we are to answer him. Bluntly stated, we answer him because real Christians don't let foolish atheists go to hell. Not without a fight.

"See a man wise in his own conceit? There is more hope of a fool than of him" (Proverbs 26:12).

FULL OF MISTAKES

From Martin James: "I was unable to find your definition of atheist in the dictionary. Did you make it up? If we're redefining words here we're going to run into problems communicating."

Martin, I find it interesting that you appeal to the absolute authority of the dictionary. Wasn't it written by men? Don't men make mistakes? Aren't there all sorts of different versions? Which one is right? Hasn't it changed down through the ages? Besides, who are they to say what's right and what's wrong when it comes to word definitions? There are no verbal absolutes. Everyone to his own. However, I think we can still communicate.

"The mouth of the righteous speaks wisdom, and his tongue talks of judgment" (Psalm 37:30).

THE MOST BRILLIANT CHRISTIAN
IS THE ONE WHO LETS HIS
LIGHT SHINE.

WHY THE TREMBLING?

A pastor was once seen pacing as he was preparing to deliver his sermon. When asked by members of his congregation if he was nervous, he answered, "Always. But it's not you. It's Him." Those who fear God show themselves to be true and faithful witnesses. They preach the fear of the Lord because they live in the fear the Lord; something the Bible calls "the beginning of wisdom." We need more men in the pulpit who tremble when they preach His Word, because the fear of God is contagious. May He give them to us while there is still time.

"The fear of the Lord is the beginning of wisdom: a good understanding have all they that do his commandments: his praise endures for ever" (Psalm 111:10).

ONE SOWS—ANOTHER REAPS

I have often joked about how candy companies are secretly owned by Weight-Watchers. If one didn't exist, there would be no need for the other. The principle is common in much of contemporary society. Similarly, the fast-food folks feed the fitness industry. Customers pay to get fat, and then they pay more to get fit. And what's more, both industries provide jobs.

Think of how much employment other popular industries provide. Cigarette manufacturers supply employment for tobacco farmers, printers, advertisers, cancer doctors, oxygen tank suppliers, heart and lung surgeons, and undertakers. Alcohol companies supply work for bottle-makers, can manufacturers, printers, advertisers, doctors, liver transplant surgeons, undertakers, marriage counselors, tow truck drivers, ambulance drivers, nurses, drug manufacturers, mental institutions, the Betty Ford Clinic, the police, and, of course, most of the court and prison system.

Hollywood had it right. It is a mad, mad world, and it's full of insane people who are intent on self-destruction. I'm so looking forward to a new Heaven and the New Earth, where the insanity will stop.

> *"... do you not know that the friendship of the world is enmity with God? Whosoever therefore will be a friend of the world is the enemy of God"* (James 4:4).

Memory Bank

Can you recall your very first memory? Mine was as a four-year-old in kindergarten. We had to line up for a class photograph and as I was the shortest, I was taken to the front and made to sit cross-legged, holding the class sign. I find the subject of memory banks incredibly fascinating. In a second, I can withdraw memories from the bank and re-spend them. Smells, songs, or something I see can trigger a pleasant or a painful memory.

Of course, like so many things we take for granted, the memory process is truly amazing. Think of a pleasant memory. Perhaps it's your house as a child. If you close your eyes and concentrate enough, you can actually walk through the door of your old house, into the kitchen, down the hall, into your

bedroom, and look at things, all within the corridors of your mind.

There's also a fearful side to this. The memory has also recorded every sin we have ever committed. Yet, as a Christian, I thank God that He knows nothing about them. The Bible says that He has forgotten my sins. However, there is the thought that if God is all-knowing, then He will know exactly what He has forgotten.

So the only way we can reconcile His forgetting with His omniscience is to realize that He has annihilated our sins, through the blood of Christ. They no longer exist. Psalm 103:12 says, "As far as the east is from the west, so far has he removed our transgressions from us." They have been removed as far as the east is from the west. That's an infinite distance. If I am at the South Pole and head north, I will eventually hit the North Pole. But if I head toward the east, I will never find the west. It's in the opposite direction. So, because of the Cross, the sins of those who trust in Jesus are at an infinite distance from the mind of God. Praise the Lord for that. Now that's a massive understatement.

"... for I will forgive their iniquity, and I will remember their sin no more" (Jeremiah 31:34).

SOME MINOR DETAILS

My heart goes out to people with bad back pain. I had it for years, but by the grace of God I found something that fixed it. Completely. I purchased some plastic shoe inserts through a TV infomercial, and to my surprise they worked.

Now I want to tell others with back pain, so that they won't have to suffer. My heart also goes out to those who suffer from insomnia. After years of lying awake at night, by the grace of God I figured out how to induce sleep. Now I want to tell others about it so that they won't suffer from insomnia. I even wrote a book about it. (*Overcoming Insomnia*, published by Bridge-Logos Publishers.)

Then again, you could get a drug that promises to help you get to sleep. The manufacturers assure the potential buyer that it really works; however, there are some possible minor side effects. They use a kind-sounding and soothing male voice in their advertisement to give these minor details: "Sleep walking and eating or driving while not fully awake, with amnesia for the event have been reported ... [it] may cause severe allergic reaction such as swelling of your tongue or throat or shortness of breath [suffocation]. If you experience any of these reactions contact your doctor [or undertaker] immediately. Other side effects may include next day drowsiness, dizziness, and headache ... and has some risk of dependency." (Brackets mine.)

My heart also goes out to people who are in their sins, hopelessly waiting to die. Back on April 25, 1972, I found the complete answer. I turned from my sins and put my trust in Jesus Christ as Lord and Savior. Now, by the grace of God, I have everlasting life, and want to tell the world.

"And they said, Believe on the Lord Jesus Christ, and you shall be saved, and your house" (Acts 16:31).

THE PARKING SPOT

A Los Angeles woman was battling an insurance company to pay for an operation to save her daughter. As she held a news conference, she was informed that the insurance company had suddenly decided to pay for the operation, so she cried out, "God is with me!" Sadly, the approval came too late; a short time later the daughter tragically died.

It reminded me of a lesson I learned as a new Christian. I had prayed for a parking spot and when someone pulled out of one in the next instant, I took it as a healthy token that God was with me, and said, "Praise the Lord!" Suddenly, someone beat me to the parking space. It was a good lesson—never take what is perceived as a positive answer to prayer as a sign that God is with us.

In John 11:32, it seemed to Mary that Jesus didn't care when He failed to respond immediately to help her ailing brother. If our faith in God is dependent on positive answers to prayer, it won't be long until we become disillusioned. When Paul lists the trials that often come to the Christian (see Romans 8:35), he concludes by saying that we are more than conquerors "through Him that loved us." That's a direct reference to the Cross. He loved us. The Cross is the lighthouse of His love, and that's where we find our stability. It shines as the evident token of God's love; that He is with all those who repent and trust the Savior. It is that knowledge that will keep us off the rocks of despair, during life's greatest storms.

"And that he might reconcile both to God in one body by the cross, having slain the enmity thereby" (Ephesians 2:16).

CIRCLE OF FUTILITY

Those who reject "In the beginning," leave themselves with no beginning, no end, and no reason to be in-between.

"Blessed is the man that trusts in the Lord, and whose hope the Lord is' (Jeremiah 17:7).

THE ATHEIST'S HOPE

When it is pointed out to an atheist that it's his obligation to provide information as to why he believes God doesn't exist, he will be quick to say that he can't do it. The best he can do is hope that God doesn't exist.

"Who by him do believe in God, that raised him up from the dead, and gave him glory; that your faith and hope might be in God" (1 Peter 1:21).

CRAZY PILOT

In December, 2007, a family of four was lost in freezing snow in the mountains of California. After three days of searching, a helicopter pilot spotted the word "Help" that had been stomped into the snow. He swooped down and rescued them.

Imagine if they had frozen to death instead, and at the inquest, the pilot said that he had seen the word in the snow,

and had come to the conclusion that it was a product of the snowstorm. Imagine if he said that he believed that random chance had formed the letters. The man would be immediately, and rightly, declared mentally unstable.

The most simple-minded human being, as opposed to unreasoning beasts, must always conclude that an intelligent message has been written by an intelligent mind. The discovery of the language of DNA should immediately convert every reasoning human being into believing that creation has intelligent design. However, we are warned in Scripture that there is such a thing as "unreasonable" men (see 2 Thessalonians 3:1-3). It is a sad testimony to the lack of human intelligence, when such blatant unreasonableness by some in the community is interpreted by the world to actually be intellectual.

"Finally, brethren, pray for us, that the word of the lord may have free course, and be glorified, even as it is with you. And that we may be delivered from unreasonable and wicked men: for all men have not faith" (2 Thessalonians 3:1-2).

TOUGH TIME?

Are you going through a tough time? We pray for deliverance, and sometimes circumstances change for the better. But sometimes they get worse. Sometimes Lazarus dies. But in the midst of what seems like a tragedy, the Christian possesses something very special, a secret consolation. Let me remind you of it by asking a question: have you ever had a song in your mind that you can't seem to shake? Now and then I get one that plays over and over in my head (there must be a "repeat" mode in there). Sometimes it's even on "play" from the moment I wake up in the morning.

One such song was from the 1960's. The words were, "You don't have to say you love me, just be close at hand. You don't have to stay 'forever,' I will understand. Believe me, believe me...."

It reminded me of our secret consolation. God didn't have to say He loved us, but He did through the Cross. He is always close at hand no matter in what lion's den we find ourselves. He will never, ever forsake us and this relationship is forever. May we fully understand this truth. All we have to do is believe Him. Believe Him. It all comes down to trust and obey, for there's no other way. I feel another song coming on....

> *"Trust in the Lord with all your heart; and lean not unto your own understanding. In all your ways acknowledge him, and he shall direct your paths"* (Proverbs 3:5-6).

MUSICAL LAWS

Do you ever think about music? I don't mean in an emotional sense. I mean objectively. Most of us never give it any depth of thought. It's just there, and we use it for our pleasure. But I would like you to give it some thought, right now. Sing a tune. Any tune. Go on. I will wait for a minute while you think of one ... got it? Okay. Now, consider the fact that you, I assume, started singing in the right key. That key is essential to the melody, because without it you will open a door that those around you will want to close quickly. Think now of the beat of the tune. It has a law of consistency to it. It may be slow or fast, but it is steady, and each beat is connected to its predecessor. It's a law of synchronization. As you sing, you are also, presumably, keeping the tune. Think now of the variety of differing harmonies that can come alongside the tune, and yet the music still remains in one accord.

How incredibly amazing to think that God created this invisible thing we call music. His unspeakable genius is seen in the laws that govern it. Without those laws, we don't have music. We simply have noise. Like this mystical thing called fire, music lies dormant until we light its warm and wonderful spark. The more I think of this amazing creation in which we live, the more I am awestruck beyond words by its amazing Creator.

> *"Praise him with the sound of the trumpet: praise him with the psaltery and harp. Praise him with the timbrel and dance: praise him with stringed instruments and organs. Praise him upon the loud cymbals: praise him upon the high sounding cymbals. Let every thing that has breath praise the Lord. Praise the Lord"* (Psalm 150:3-6).

Reversing a Curse

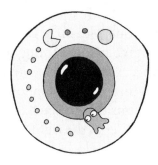

Do you get "floaters"? They are very common. They are small shadows on the eyeball that move when the eye is moved. I have had them now and then over the years, but I got one that stayed some time ago. When I asked around, I found that they are very common. Someone even told me that he had so many floaters he would often play a kind of PAC-MAN when he had nothing to do. I'm not at that level as yet. Mine is at a point where I still jump out of my skin because I see a spider on a wall to my right, or a fly, or two cursors on the screen of my laptop.

Floaters can be a little annoying, but I have turned the curse into a blessing. Whenever I see mine, I have programed myself to use it as an alarm clock for me to pray that God raises up laborers who will seek the lost. Maybe you have annoying things in your life, *persistent floaters that suddenly show up in front of your eyes. Don't let them get you* down. Rather, let them get you to prayer. Turn a curse into a blessing.

> *"In every thing give thanks: for this is the will of God in Christ Jesus concerning you"* (1 Thessalonians 5:18).

The Problem of Drooling

After our dog died, we decided we wouldn't get another one. That is, until I spotted a man who was leashed to a Great Dane, who had a small crowd gathered around him. Most of the people were patting the dog and chatting with the man. I immediately saw great evangelistic potential in the situation. If I had a Great Dane, I would have an instant bridge to reach out to the unsaved. I could even print up a dog tract, using the cream of an unpublished book called, *101 Things Dogs Do to Annoy Their Owners*.

When I mentioned this to a friend, he said that he could have a saddle made for me. That's the positive side. Here's the negative: 1. Drooling—I would get one of those sucking things that dentists use and hook it up to his collar. 2. Shedding—he stays outside during the day. 3. Barking—an anti-bark collar. Then there is the small problem of Sue being horrified at the thought. Maybe it's the dilemma of how much room he would take up in our bed at night. I had better think on it.

"But let patience have her perfect work, that you may be perfect and entire, wanting nothing" (James 1:4).

THE CHARACTER OF GOD

Someone asked me if it were true that God is our enemy before we come to Christ. There is no argument that we are enemies of God. The Scriptures tell us that we are enemies in mind (see Colossians 1:21), and if we are a friend of the world, we are an enemy of God (see James 4:4). So, it's clear that we are enemies of God, but is He an enemy to us?

The Bible tells us that when we were in our sins His wrath hovered over us (see John 3:36), and every time we sinned, we stored up further wrath (see Romans 2:5). The fullness of His fury is going to be revealed on the Day of Wrath, in which He will give "tribulation and anguish" to the disobedient (see Romans 2:8-9). Colossians 3:6 calls humanity "children of disobedience" upon whom will come "flaming fire" and "everlasting destruction" (see 2 Thessalonians 1:7-10).

So there's not exactly a state of peace between Heaven and us. We are at war. So is God our enemy? To answer that, ask yourself if a good judge is the enemy of a vicious, murderous rapist who stands before him in court. In a judicial sense, he is.

The judge is furious at the man, and he will discharge his wrath through the path of justice.

In these days where God's disposition is characterized as one of passive benevolence, and He is therefore everyone's buddy, it is essential that our preaching reveals His true character as portrayed in Scripture. He is the ultimate righteous and just Judge. He is wrath-filled, and He has appointed death as an officer of the Law that will eventually arrest the guilty. He will charge them with crimes against the Law, and it is those crimes that will take humanity to the prison of hell and slam the door. What a fearful thing.

However, there is a huge difference between those who are our human enemies and a holy God. When Jesus told us to love our enemies, He said "… that you may be children of your father in Heaven: for He makes the sun rise on the evil and the good, and sends rain on the just and the unjust" (Matthew 5:44-45). That love was ultimately expressed at the Cross.

"For God sent not his Son into the world to condemn the world; but that the world through him might be saved" (John 3:17).

Respectful Person

A note from a critic, "I yust want to complain that Kurt Cameron said on a comercial on Gospel Channel that i`m not a good person yust becose i dont belive in God. yust becose you guys dont know what your talking aboat, and i happend to know something aboat the world around me, that maykes me to a bad person?? i respekt every humans, something you do not. if a person dont belive in God, they are not good inof. but i even try to respekt you, but it is not easy when you dont respekt me. i respeckt all people and al life. but i dont belive in God, becose i see the world as it is, i understand more then all of you relegius people. but that dont mayke me to a bad person. And based on that, what you stand for, is discriminating. and you call your self good people? non of you know the meaning of it."

"Judge not, that you be not judged" (Matthew 7:1).

HARK, THE HERALD ANGELS SING

Addendum Version:
Hark the herald angels sing,
"Glory to the newborn King!"
Peace on Earth and mercy mild
God and sinners reconciled.
Joyful, all ye nations rise,
What will happen when you die?
Will you go to Heaven or hell?
Jesus knows! Emmanuel.
Hark! The herald angels sing,
"Glory to the newborn King!"

Christ by highest Heav'n adored,
Christ, the everlasting Lord!
He's the One who'll judge us all,
Let's see who will stand or fall …
Have you ever told a lie?
Wished that someone else would die?
Entertained a lusty thought?
Stolen when you should have bought?
Help! We've broken God's ten laws!
Who will come to save us all?

That's why Jesus Christ was sent,
To be saved you must repent.

Died on the Cross for all your sin,
Repent and put your trust in Him.
Mild He laid His glory by,
Born that man no more may die,
Born to raise the sons of Earth,
Born to give them second birth,
Hark! The herald angels sing,
"Glory to the newborn King!"

> *"And suddenly there was with the angel a multitude
> of the heavenly host praising God, and saying, Glory
> to God in the highest, and on earth peace, good will
> toward men"* (Luke 2:13-14).

CHOCOLATE LOVERS

I'm the world's biggest skeptic when it comes to what *experts* tell us. One moment they are saying that alcohol is a killer, and the next they are saying it's the best thing since sliced bread. Yeah, sure. Or they say that being overweight is bad; then it's good. Yep. Sure. Their studies have driven me into hardened cynicism.

I heard one expert say that dark chocolate is good for us. Wha …! Good for us! Huh? He said what? The expert maintained that it contains flavonoids that are in antioxidants, and they are associated with reduced risk of heart disease, reduced risk of injury to blood vessels, reduced risk of diabetes, reduced risk of stroke, and reduced risk of cancer. I realized that I'd had a bad attitude. I turned from it, and became a believer in what the expert said … and faith without works is dead.

"But will you know, O vain man, that faith without works is dead?" (James 2:20).

THE NATIONS

In Psalm 9:20, David prays, "Put them in fear, O Lord: that the nations may know themselves to be but men." We tend to forget that great nations are made up of human beings that brush their teeth with one brush at a time. Each politically prominent person is just a man or woman "whose breath is in his (or her) nostrils." (See Isaiah 2:22.) If God was to invisibly place His holy hand over our noses and mouths, it would be curtains for us, no matter how big the show. Jesus spoke of a man that God said He would snuff out. He said to him, "Tonight your soul is required of you." We are like a small candle on a very big cake. God is the one who gives the sparks to our lives and He is the One who puts out the flame, despite the natural circumstances that may surround our demise. The world speaks of and trembles at the thought of the Grim Reaper. We know better. Jesus told us whom to fear.

"And fear not them which kill the body, but are not able to kill the soul: but rather fear him which is able to destroy both soul and body in hell" (Matthew 10:28).

How's Your General Knowledge?

Who came up with the powerful words: "Ask not what your country can do for you—ask what you can do for your country"? If you answered that it was John Fitzgerald Kennedy, who spoke these words during his 1961 inaugural speech, you would be wrong. It was President Kennedy's speechwriter—probably a Mr. Theodore Sorenson, who was the president's chief speechwriter at the time. Even though it takes skill to deliver, something doesn't quite sit with me when I find out that  politicians actually read someone else's words in their speeches and that famous comedians don't write their own jokes; they buy them.

Here's another question for you. This one is about Bible knowledge. Who wrote the Book of Romans? If you said that it was the Apostle Paul, sorry, you are wrong. He was tied up at the time, so he spoke the entire epistle to Tertius, who wrote it down (see Romans 16:22). So I guess Tertius was also a speechwriter. But, come to think of it, even he can't take the credit. He had a Ghostwriter.

"I Tertius, who wrote this epistle, salute you in the Lord" (Romans 16:22).

Value Your Life

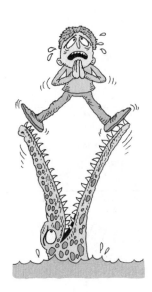

There's a new documentary that asks the question, "Is the risk worth the reward?" It's about base-jumping and other extreme sports, where people put their lives on the line for the excitement of the adrenaline rush. I'm taking a risk here in saying this, but I answer that question with, "No. Absolutely not." Never, ever risk your precious, God-given life for anything but the gospel.

I have seen a number of extreme sports documentaries where a jumper ignores his self-preserving fear for the excitement of the risk. At the very end of the documentary, it's disclosed that the person was tragically killed in a recent jump. I wonder what his last thoughts were about the risk-versus-pleasure question, just before he hit the ground. I wonder what the thoughts were of those who picked up the bloody, smashed body of the dead thrill-seeker. If you want an adrenaline rush, simply preach in the open air, and if you are stoned to death for it, eternity will show that the risk was well worth the reward.

"Hereby perceive we the love of God, because he laid down his life for us: and we ought to lay down our lives for the brethren" (1 John 3:16).

Two Tasks

I am always encouraged when I read the writings of men or women of the past who used the same analogies and seemed to feel the same frustrations we do when it comes to reaching the lost. Thomas Watson, way back in 1660, wrote of something he called "cruel mercy." He quoted Jude 23: "… rescue others by snatching them from the fire," and then said,  "If a man's house were on fire, and another should see it and not tell him of it, for fear of waking him—would not this be cruelty? When we see others sleeping in their sin, and the fire of God's wrath ready to burn them up—and we are silent—is not this cruelty?"

All around us we have professed firefighters who prefer to stay in the comfort of the fire station and let people burn. So you and I have a two-fold task: the first is to awaken those within the Church to their sober responsibility to reach out to the unsaved, and the second is to reach out to those who are ignorant as to their true state before God. Perhaps the two tasks are one in the same.

"Go therefore, and teach all nations, baptizing them in the name of the Father, and of the Son, and of the Holy Spirit" (Matthew 28:19).

Moses Knows

I have been reading The Amplified Bible to Sue for our nightly readings for the past year. The neighbors will be pleased when I'm finished. (It's The Amplified Bible, so it should be read a little louder than most).

The other night I read: "Put out of your minds the thought and do not suppose [as some of you are supposing] that I will accuse you before the Father. There is one who accuses you—it is Moses, the very one on whom you have built your hopes [in whom you trust]. For if you believed and relied on Moses, you would believe and rely on Me, for he wrote about Me [personally]. But if you do not believe and trust his writings, how then will you believe and trust My teachings? [How shall you cleave to and rely on My words?]" (John 5:45-47).

Often those who are opposed to biblical evangelism say that Jesus didn't go around condemning sinners. They are right. He didn't need to. He used the Law of Moses (see Mark 10:17-19, among other references) because, as He says in this passage, it is the Law of Moses that accuses. It points its ten indignant fingers at sinners and leaves them guilty before the judgment bar of a holy God. Those who are persuaded by the Law and understand their sinful and condemned condition will flee to the Savior for mercy. Those who don't, won't.

"And Jesus said to him, Why do you call me good? There is none good but one, that is, God. You know the commandments, Do not commit adultery, Do not kill, Do not steal, Do not bear false witness, Defraud not, Honor your father and mother" (Mark 10:18-19).

GO TO THE ANT

If you have trouble with laziness, overeating, lust (the usual sins that so easily beset us), or depression, here's a principle that may help you: weeds don't grow on a busy footpath. We are often most vulnerable to these sinful weeds when we are idle. So, do something that will keep your mind occupied; other than eat, that is.

Here's a suggestion: use the Internet and type in search words that are going to get you talking to the unsaved. Words such as: "I don't know if God exists," "I don't believe in God," "Is God real?" "Who was Jesus?" "I don't like religion," "I'm afraid of dying." Think of other words and phrases that will find some lost person, and simply ask them questions such as, "Why do you feel like that?" Before you know it, you will be running to check their responses to your questions. You can build up a file of answers that you can paste into your emails. They are for those who are offended by "religion" or can't see any evidence of God's existence.

To build up a file, go to www.evidencebible.com. There you will find one hundred of the most commonly asked questions of the Christian faith, plus a lot more. You may cut and paste these free of charge.

"But sanctify the Lord God in your hearts: and be ready always to give an answer to every man that asks you a reason of the hope that is in you with meekness and fear" (1 Peter 3:15).

BUG YOUR DOCTOR

Scotty is the soundman for our radio program. He sits a lot at his computer and wanted to exercise more, so I encouraged him to take my bike and ride it during his lunch hour. Meanwhile, I had an appointment with my doctor to get my yearly checkup. I like my doctor. The first time we met, he seemed to spend ages looking into my left ear. Then he stood in front of me and said, "I want you to firmly pull down on the earlobe." So I reached out, grabbed his earlobe, and pulled down firmly. His face lit up like a man whose face lit up. He laughed and laughed. It was then that I realized that this poor man, even though he was a Christian, had a pretty sad life. People who visit him are usually miserable and complaining about something. So I determined to lift his spirits whenever I could.

I arrived at the doctor's office, we greeted each other, and then I unbuttoned my shirt and lay on the examination table. Hidden in my hand was a two-inch, lifelike plastic cockroach. I took one to my dentist a few years back. When he told me to open my mouth, there it was, sitting on my tongue. He sure freaked out. There was something deeply gratifying about giving my dentist a little pain.

So, as my doctor checked my heart, I skillfully slipped the roach onto my stomach. It took a second, but boy, did he jump! Then he laughed and laughed. After the examination he just sat there and made small talk. He was either thoroughly enjoying the fellowship, or he was secretly conducting a psychological examination.

I got back to the ministry and found that Scotty did go for a ride on my bike. He was quietly riding down the street, when suddenly something shot out from a driveway. It was a canine cannonball! Scotty found himself being chased by the crazed, demon-possessed, hate-filled, anti-Christ Chihuahua that had been hounding me for weeks. The mad dog must have thought it was me on the bike. Yes, Scotty is strikingly handsome. He said that the "little rat" scared the living daylights out of him, and he peddled so fast he burned off three pounds.

"A merry heart does good like a medicine: but a broken spirit dries the bones" (Proverbs 17:22).

Arizona Atheist

The problem with the subject of evolution is that it is full of time-wasting rabbit trails. Here is an example of one. My evolutionist friend said that there are plenty of transitional forms, and he cut and pasted some examples for me:

He said, "Hi ... a few come to mind immediately, and they are named as follows: Tiktaalik roseae, Acanthostega, Ichthyostega, Archaeopteryx, and Homo rudolfensis, just to name a few.

For more information about many more fossils, here is a good page to visit: http://www.talkorigins.org/faqs/faq-transitional.html."

ARCHAEOPTERYX

Bird's brain shape and size

Bird's feathers

Bird's feathered tail

Bird's upper and lower beak

Bird's strong furcula (wishbone)

Bird's grasping hallux (hind toe)

Bird's thin light and strong bones

VERDICT: A true bird and not some transitional form.

That's your positive proof. Now my job is to answer all this evidence you have given, so let's deal with "Archaeopteryx."

Was Archaeopteryx a feathered dinosaur? Dr. Alan Feduccia, a world authority on birds at the University of North Carolina at Chapel Hill and an evolutionist himself, said: "Paleontologists have tried to turn Archaeopteryx into

171

an earth-bound, feathered dinosaur. But it's not. It is a bird, a perching bird. And no amount of 'paleobabble' is going to change that."

I don't have time to go down your other rabbit trails, but I will address your: "For more information about many more fossils, here is a good page to see: http://www.talkorigins.org/faqs/faq-transitional.html."

Here is your "information" from that site (it's in italics to differentiate it from my words):

Part 1

The term "transitional fossil" is used at least two different ways on talk.origins, often leading to muddled and stalemated arguments. I call these two meanings the "general lineage" and the "species-to-species transition."

"General lineage":

This is a sequence of similar genera or families, linking an older group to a very different younger group. Each step in the sequence consists of some fossils that represent a certain genus or family, and the whole sequence often covers a span of tens of millions of years. A lineage like this shows obvious morphological intermediates for every major structural change, and the fossils occur roughly (but often not exactly) in the expected order. Usually there are still gaps between each of the groups—few or none of the speciation events are preserved. Sometimes the individual specimens are not thought to be directly ancestral to the next-youngest fossils (i.e., they may be "cousins" or "uncles" rather than "parents"). However, they are assumed to be closely related to the actual ancestor, since they have intermediate morphology compared to the next-oldest and next-youngest "links." The major point of these general lineages is that animals with intermediate morphology existed at the appropriate times, and thus that the transitions from the proposed ancestors are fully plausible. General lineages are known for almost all modern groups of vertebrates, and make up the bulk of this FAQ.

General lineage has nothing to do with macro-evolution at all, or one species evolving into another.

"Species-to-species transition":
This is a set of numerous individual fossils that show a change between one species and another. It's a very fine-grained sequence documenting the actual speciation event, usually covering less than a million years. These species-to-species transitions are unmistakable when they are found. Throughout successive strata you see the population averages of teeth, feet, vertebrae, etc., changing from what is typical of the first species to what is typical of the next species. Sometimes, these sequences occur only in a limited geographic area (the place where the speciation actually occurred), with analyses from any other area showing an apparently "sudden" change. Other times, though, the transition can be seen over a very wide geological area. Many "species-to-species transitions" are known, mostly for marine invertebrates and recent mammals (both those groups tend to have good fossil records), though they are not as abundant as the general lineages (see below for why this is so). Part 2 lists numerous species-to-species transitions from the mammals.
"1. 'The FAQ doesn't have real transitional fossils.' If you have just skimmed part of the FAQ and concluded that it doesn't have what you consider to be "real" transitional fossils, go back to part 1 of the FAQ and carefully read the section titled "What is a transitional fossil?" Think about what you have read. Then read the rest of the FAQ, and pay particular attention to the "species-to-species" sections in part 2. If you still think the FAQ doesn't have "real" transitional fossils, chances are you have misunderstood the theory of evolution. Define what a "real" transitional fossil should be, and why you think the modern theory of evolution would predict such a thing. Then let's talk."
http://www.talkorigins.org/faqs/faq-transitional/email.html

The reason that "many 'species-to-species transitions' are known though they are not as abundant as the general lineages," is that there aren't any. There are no transitional fossils (species-to-species transitions). Anyone who thinks there are has "misunderstood the theory of evolution."

I am done. Look at all the time and trouble I had to go to, to unravel the quick knot you tied with your "evidence." So, please don't cut and paste any more evidence and send it to me. If you want, I can send you a free copy of *Evolution—a Fairy Tale for Grownups*. It is packed with quotes from evolution "experts" who admit that they don't have anything but a ripe imagination.

I appreciate the fact that you said in an unpublished email that you don't consider me to be your "friend." That's my loss.

May God continue to bless you and your family,
Ray

"For by him were all things created, that are in heaven, and that are in earth, visible and invisible, whether they be thrones, or dominions, or principalities, or powers: all things were created by him, and for him" (Colossians 1:16).

THE BIG THREE

What is it that keeps most people from coming to Christ? That question probably has a three-fold answer: 1. Pride, 2. Love for sin, and 3. A lack of knowledge. The Bible tells us, "The wicked, for the pride of his countenance, will not seek after God" (Psalm 10:4). Sin and pride are intertwined. We puff our rebellious chests against the heavens and say, "Who is God to tell me what to do?" There's no fear of God before our eyes.

The reason we don't fear Him is because we lack knowledge. We cling to our image of God like a child clings to his security blanket, and if you have ever tried to separate a child from his

blanket, you will know what a hard job that is. But that's what we must do. With the help of God, we must separate the sinner from his idol. And the way to do that is to preach the Commandments, as Jesus did.

The moral Law makes the issue clear. God is holy, and He will not tolerate sin in any form, nor will He tolerate any other gods before Him. That's right; God is politically incorrect. He is uncompromisingly intolerant. Hell will prove that. The light of the Law not only exposes idolatry, but it humbles the sinner, and gives him the knowledge that without the grace of God, he will perish. So never despise God's Law, and never neglect it when heralding the glorious Cross.

"The fear of the Lord is the beginning of wisdom: and the knowledge of the holy is understanding" (Proverbs 9:10).

Brain Squeeze

Here's a question to test your general knowledge. What was the name of the world's highest peak before Mount Everest was discovered? Do you know? Of course you do. It was Mount Everest. It was the world's highest mountain even before we found it. What we once thought was the highest peak, wasn't. New knowledge changed our beliefs.

It is because of this principle that science can never be absolutely certain

of anything. It can only believe something according to the knowledge it has at present. And even when it gets more knowledge, it still can't be absolutely certain it has the truth, because future information may refute what it thinks it knows to be true. What science believes now may be laughed at in one hundred years' time.

Some think that's a good thing, because it shows that science is forever open to change. The only good thing about it is that is shows us where we should put our trust. God alone speaks absolute truth, because He has absolute knowledge. Science can never say that something is a fact. God can and does. That's why we can have absolute trust about anything He says in His Word. It's as solid as a rock (*solider*, if there's such a word). Those that trust in Him need never be disappointed, disillusioned, or discouraged. And that's a fact.

> *"For the word of God is quick, and powerful, and sharper than any two-edged sword, piercing even to the dividing asunder of soul and spirit, and of the joints and marrow, and is a discerner of the thoughts and intents of the heart"* (Hebrews 4:12).

Great Books

Are you familiar with the writings of Peter Johnson? I love his books, and for many years I have enjoyed reading them regularly. There is something refreshing about an author who tells it like it is, and Johnson does just that, in a uniquely powerful and inspired way. As far as I know, he authored only two books in his entire lifetime, and both of them were published after his death.

But I find myself going back to them again and again because each time I turn the pages, it's as though it's my first time. That is very special. Sadly, he was viciously murdered in his old age, but as a young man he lived on the edge, and his colorful life has become an inspiration for countless people.

I'm sure you are familiar with his writings. If you are not, it would be good to get some background information before you open them. You can read about his early life by opening the New Testament at John 1:42, where most translations tell us he was originally called "Simon, son of John" before his name was changed to "Peter, son of John," or "Peter Johnson," as he would now be known.

> *"And he brought him to Jesus. And when Jesus beheld him, he said, You are Simon the son of Jonah: you shall be called Cephas, which is by interpretation, A stone"* (John 1:42).

Something Important

I was talking to someone on my cell phone when someone else tried to get through. It may have been something important, so I quickly finished the call I was on, and switched to the next one. It was strange. There was no one there. I must have cut them off. I checked the number, and saw that it was someone from our ministry. It may have been Sue, wanting to tell me something important, so I called her.

While I was waiting for her to answer, another call came through. I abandoned the call to Sue and took the incoming one. It was EZ, my son-in-law. He asked why his call to me went dead. I said that I didn't know what happened. Suddenly someone else was trying to get through. I told him to wait while I checked the incoming call, as it might be Sue wanting to tell me something important. It was her, so I asked what she wanted. She didn't want anything. She was asking why I called her a minute earlier. I said that I thought that she had called me, but it was actually EZ, who was waiting on the other line and maybe he had something important to tell me. She said goodbye, and I switched back to EZ.

He wasn't there. I then called his land line, but all I got was his voice mail telling me he wasn't there. So I called his cell phone. He took my call, but couldn't talk because while he was waiting for me to get back to him, he had taken a call from his sister, who was on the other line. He said that it was about something important.

"But let patience have her perfect work, that you may be perfect and entire, wanting nothing" (James 1:4).

HAPPY HOLIDAY AND ALL THAT

Some folk get upset when businesses avoid saying, "Merry Christmas!" at Christmas time. Instead, they have changed the greeting to "Happy Holiday!" I don't know whether they are trying to be politically correct or if they are deliberately trying to get Christ out of Christmas. Whatever the case, they should check out what they are saying. The origin of the word "holiday," according to the dictionary, is "holy day," from Old English. There's enough spark of truth left in the word for us to remind this world that Christmas truly is a holy day. So don't let the word upset you. Let it set you up.

"And she shall bring forth a son, and you shall call his name JESUS: for he shall save his people from their sins" (Matthew 1:21).

Sleeping Beauty?

Sleep sure shows us that we live in what the Bible calls a fallen state. It totally strips a man of his control, and of his dignity. Whether he's a king or a pauper, sleep casts him into a deep sea of unpredictability. Inside, his mind drifts like a ship without a rudder or anchor, from pleasure to terror in an instant. Outside, sleep opens his mouth, and from that undignified chasm he sends out noises reminiscent of a disgusting pig with his face in filthy fodder.

Time magazine asks, "Is [sleep] to refresh the body? Not really. Researchers have yet to find any vital biological function that sleep restores.... Is it to refresh the mind? That's closer to the mark. The brain benefits from a good night's sleep. But there is no agreement among sleep researchers about what form that benefit takes."

Then again, God may have just given it to us as something to do until the sun comes up. Whatever the case, the Bible tells us that we shouldn't love sleep. We should get what we need and then use our waking hours to do the will of Him who woke us from our deathly stupor, and gave us glorious light. "Therefore He says: 'Awake, you who sleep, arise from the dead, and Christ will give you light'" (Ephesians 5:14).

"You are all the children of light, and the children of the day: we are not of the night, nor of darkness. Therefore let us not sleep, as do others; but let us watch and be sober" (1 Thessalonians 5:5-6).

THE MYSTERY OF FIRE

Do you ever think about fire? What is this mysterious thing that needs fuel to survive? When it's under control, fire works for our benefit. It gives us the pleasure of warmth, light, and the ability to heat up vegetable soup. When it's out of control, it becomes a terrifying inferno. Fire isn't something that was accidentally discovered by some primal caveman. God gave it to humanity for our benefit.

It's like His gift of sex. Keep it under the control of righteousness, and it will give you pleasure. Let it get out of control through lust and pornography, and it will eventually overtake you. You end up at its mercy. It will start as a warm and harmless glow, but there is a demonic wind that will blow the flame until it is out of control, and it will demand fuel to survive. You become its fuel.

Look at this warning: For by means of a whorish woman a man is brought to a piece of bread: and the adulteress will hunt for the precious life. Can a man take fire in his bosom, and his clothes not be burned? Can one go upon hot coals, and his feet not be burned? (Proverbs 6:26-28)

So, what is the answer for moth-brained men, who just can't keep away from the fascinating flame? It is to put it out through repentance toward the God we have offended, and through absolute trust in the One who suffered and died to make us clean. Then we can keep the fire out daily, with the washing of the water of the Word.

"That he might sanctify and cleanse it with the washing of water by the word" (Ephesians 5:26).

SURVIVAL EXPERTISE

After a high-rise window-washer in New York, a skydiver, and a skate-boarder all cheated death after falling, an expert said, "Our DNA is coded to survive." In other words, God has placed in each of us a will to live—my words, not his. No one in his or her right mind wants to die. Then the expert said, "Every survival expert, no matter what the situation, tells you that surviving comes down to three basic things. Number One, [be] prepared; Number Two, don't panic; and Number Three, have a plan."

In other words, if you are a skydiver, first think about what you would do if your parachute malfunctioned. Second, if it happens, don't let fear take away clear thinking, and third, from that point do what you can to get yourself safely back on the Earth.

Here now is your eternal survival plan. First, be prepared to face a holy God. Second, think clearly about your many sins, and what you are going to do to justify yourself so that you will escape the damnation of hell. And third, put your trust entirely in Jesus Christ so that you will be saved from eternal justice. That's the most expert advice you will ever get, because it comes from the Bible.

"Prepare to meet your God" (Amos 4:12).

ARIZONA ATHEIST

"I'm actually trying to save people from themselves," the Arizona Atheist says, "and people like Ray who spread falsehoods. I'm fighting for truth. If he is so truthful, why hasn't he attempted to rebut my many arguments—especially my rebuttal to his claims about me (Arizona Atheist)? Can he not answer? I'm beginning to think this is the case. Yes, Ray and many others believe in this eternal hell, but does believing make something true? Absolutely not."

Arizona Atheist, I'm sorry I didn't answer you. I have been busy. You are right, though, just believing something, doesn't make it true. The existence of God has nothing to do with whether or not I believe or whether or not you don't believe. For me, the whole issue comes down to the existence of a place called hell. If it doesn't exist, then each of us should follow every desire of our hearts, if it gives us pleasure and doesn't violate civil law. That seems to make sense, because then the door swings open to the exciting pleasures of free sex, pornography, and anything else our minds can conceive.

That's almost where our culture is at the moment. If it's the culture that sets the rules, as opposed to God, and there's no punishment after death for sin, then anything goes, as long as the law says it is permissible. That's the safety net: civil law. If the culture allows homosexuality as a morally permissible practice, then it becomes okay because there are no absolutes of right and wrong. If civil law then says pedophilia is morally acceptable, no one should object. It becomes morally okay. Everyone to his own desires.

But if civil law says it's legitimate to liquidate six million Jews, as well as blacks, homosexuals, and Gypsies, then that's also okay, because society sets the rules. Nothing is written in stone. There are no Ten Commandments to set moral boundaries, and the fact that there is no punishment for a man like Hitler means that he got away with murder, six million times over. And that's all right.

However, if there is a God, and every Christian who has truly been born again has the distinct advantage of knowing Him personally (see John 17:3), and He is good by nature, then there must be a day of justice for people who have literally gotten away with murder. Statistics tell us that there are hundreds of thousands who have done just that in America alone. The Bible warns that God is so good, He will also see to it that rapists, thieves, adulterers, fornicators, blasphemers, and liars will be punished, and the place of punishment is in a terrible place called hell. However, there are some who think that by not believing in it, it doesn't exist.

I can only tell them that they can find out the truth by repentance and faith in Jesus. Or they can wait and find the truth experientially when they die in their sins. I am horrified at the thought of that happening to my worst enemy. All I can do is plead with them, and you, before that happens. Thanks for listening to me, my friend. I will leave it up to other Christians to answer any further questions you may have.

"... the goodness of God leads you to repentance" (Romans 2:4).

THE WING-SUIT

The Bible addresses those who deny God's hand in creation by saying that they profess to be wise, but in reality, they are fools. (See Romans 1:20-22.) Take, for instance, the courageous gentleman who flies through the air in a squirrel-

suit. He and his buddies are trying to figure out how they can land without a parachute. He may do it, but listen to his explanation of how they got the design for the suit: "The wing-suit basically is fabric that goes between your arms and between your legs, and it changes the shape of your body so in essence, you become a flying squirrel. I think that's one of the amazing things about human beings, is how quickly we can evolve through technology and through using our minds [note: they copied the squirrel suit]. If you think about a flying squirrel, it took … millions of years to evolve the ability to jump from a high altitude and land uninjured."

So, he's saying that God didn't make the flying squirrel as it is. It didn't originally have the ability to fly. It had no wings, and over millions of years it began to evolve (small wings), and passed those semi-evolved-wing-thing genes onto its offspring, until we eventually ended up with the flying squirrel.

Okay, let's go with that for a moment. The first squirrel has no wings. He can't fly, but he attempts to fly through the trees and hits the ground with a terrible thud. That's what happens when you try to fly and you don't have wings. He was either seriously injured, or more than likely he died tragically. Whatever the case, his offspring also jumped without wings, and no doubt met the same fate. So did their offspring, and so did theirs. So, why would wings begin to evolve in the genes of the successive generations of un-winged squirrels, when the first and the successive flights failed miserably? Don't say that it was a case of "survival of the fittest." There were no "survivors." The flying experiment was a disaster.

However, the alternative is to say that God made flying squirrels with wings, and that's not a consideration for these folks. Evolution is an intellectual embarrassment. But that doesn't seem to matter to the believers in the fairy tale of evolution.

"And God made the beast of the earth after his kind, and cattle after their kind, and every thing that creeps upon the earth after his kind: and God saw that it was good" (Genesis 1:25).

SCIENCE HAS NO REAL ANSWER

Here's a question that science can't really answer: What is light? Of course, we know that the sun is the Earth's main source of light, and that we have other minor sources of light. We have fire, florescent light, ultraviolet light, and infrared light, just to name a few. But with all the knowledge that we have acquired through time, we know so little about this wonderful thing called "light."

Light allows us to see. It gives us warmth. It is responsible for color. It moves fairly quickly, at 186,000 miles per second. We can't take hold of it, we can't outrun it, and can't even really define it. If you look for more than a few seconds at our source of light, it will blind you. Without it, we would eventually perish. The Bible likens God to light. He gave us our sight. We can experience the warmth of His love and kindness. We can't get away from Him, and without Him we will eventually perish.

"This then is the message which we have heard of him, and declare to you, that God is light, and in him is no darkness at all" (1 John 1:5).

FANATICAL ATHEISM

It was Heywood Broun who said, "Nobody talks so constantly about God as those who insist that there is no God." There are at least two reasons for this strange phenomenon. First, the professing atheist is like a man who continually talks about his belief that infrared light doesn't exist, despite the fact that he uses it when he changes a TV channel with his remote control. Infrared light is invisible to his naked eye, so he insists on telling others that it doesn't exist.

This ties in with the second reason he talks about God so often. It is because he has no purpose for his own existence. Talking so often about God and how He doesn't exist, not only gives him a sense of identity as an atheist, but it also gives him something to do with his meaningless life until the day he dies.

He should thank God that Christians are caring enough to humble themselves intellectually, and challenge him in his beliefs. But we do because we love him ... and somehow that makes atheists mad. Human nature is both strange, and predictable.

"Beloved, if God so loved us, we ought also to love one another" (1 John 4:11).

What's in a Mustache?

Someone once looked at my face and said, "What makes your nose so important that it has to be underlined?" He made a good point. A mustache hasn't any real function. It's purely cosmetic. I have a broom-lip because my dad had one and I liked it. My son-in-law once pleaded with me to shave it off. I did, and was a little shocked to have someone say, "You don't look like Ray Comfort any more!" I didn't look like me. I looked like a pathetic, featherless sparrow. My new image didn't fly with Sue either. She made me grow it back, which provokes the question, is my identity wrapped up in my looks? This world would say that it is.

A good-looking Hollywood actor at the age of seventy looks nothing like the image that was captured when he was in his twenties. The reality of that image has gone forever. So, if we are ever changing, who or what is the real you? It is your soul, your very essence. Jesus didn't say, "What shall it profit a man if he gains the whole world and loses his own ... body." He said it's the soul that will be clothed in eternity, and it will either be clothed with glory, or corruption.

So don't spend too much time grooming that which is temporal. Build the muscle of your character.

"While we look not at the things which are seen, but at the things which are not seen: for the things which are seen are temporal; but the things which are not seen are eternal" (2 Corinthians 4:18).

THE CONSOLATION

The Bible tells us that God is holy and just and is to be feared because He has a hatred for sin. This absolute righteousness will spill over one day as terrifying and eternal wrath against all wickedness. That will be a wonderful day, but at the same time, how fearful that sounds to guilty sinners. Yet, there is an incredible consolation for us behind this terrible wrath. God is wrath-filled because of His absolute integrity. In Him is no darkness at all. He is without sin, and therefore cannot lie.

It is that pure integrity that will not only make sure that justice is done, but it will also make sure every word He has promised will be fulfilled. How unspeakably comforting that is for those who lie on a deathbed, trusting in Christ alone. All who repent and trust in Him have everlasting life and will have pleasures forevermore. That is immutable. It cannot be changed. It is both sure and steadfast, an anchor for the soul.

Those who profess to love God and yet, for some reason, dilute His wrath against sin also dilute His integrity. If He is going to compromise eternal justice in the slightest degree, He is capable of sin, and if He is capable of sin, He is capable of deceit. They, therefore, leave themselves with a non-existent idol, which cannot be trusted to keep its promises.

"Which hope we have as an anchor of the soul, both sure and steadfast, and which enters into that within the veil" (Hebrews 6:19).

THE VOCAL WOMAN

If you are a married woman and want to get pregnant, perhaps you should visit Naples, Italy, and sit in a *miracle chair*. Many pilgrims do just that, and some get pregnant. An elderly nun will wave a wooden cross over you that contains bones and hair from a bleeding and dying nun, who sat in the same chair 200 years ago. She was said to have had the five wounds of Jesus on her body, called stigmata, and when she picked up a wooden image of the baby Jesus, His folded arms unfolded. Hence, the connection with babies and pregnancy.

I guess it's not much weirder than the miracle water that is peddled by creepy Protestant evangelists on cable TV. The first seed of Catholicism may have been seen in Luke 11:27, when a woman called out to Jesus, "Blessed is the womb that bore You, and the breasts which nursed You!" Jesus didn't rebuke her for calling Mary blessed, but He did say, "…'On the contrary …'" If she wanted God's blessing on her life, she should listen to God's Word and obey it. (See Luke 11:28.)

Miracle chairs, miracle water, or hairy crosses will mean nothing on the day when God judges humanity. It is then that we will see that Jesus alone is "… the Author of eternal salvation *to all them that obey Him*" (Hebrews 5:9, italics added). However, salvation doesn't come from us being obedient to Jesus. Our obedience is the result of being given a new heart, through the new birth spoken of in the Gospel of John, chapter 3. Eternal life is the gift of God (see Ephesians 2:8-9), but those who are saved by His grace hear His voice, and run to do His will.

"For by grace are you saved through faith; and that not of yourselves: it is the gift of God: not of works, lest any man should boast" (Ephesians 2:8-9).

Not-So-Senseless Killings

There was another senseless mass killing recently. This one was in Colorado. I am hesitant to talk about it because I may sound simplistic and repetitive. I don't think the killings were senseless at all. Something is not senseless when there's a predictable pattern. Here was another disillusioned and bitter backslider, a false convert, who no doubt gave his heart to Jesus because of the promise of a wonderful new life in Christ, and when the promise didn't deliver, he was angry enough to kill. He targeted four Christians and murdered them before being shot by an armed church security guard, which is in itself a sign of the times.

My own pastor recently held up a Bible and a copy of a very popular book by "America's pastor." The publication promised God's best for you right here and now. It was another *things-go-better-with-Jesus* book, or what I call the modern gospel. My pastor said that both books were left by the church dumpster with what amounted to a suicide note scribbled in the Bible, saying that the promises of the Bible didn't match the promises of the book. How unspeakably tragic.

The world may speak well of smiley preachers who refuse to open up the Law so that sinners can see their terrible danger, but they are, in truth, betrayers of the ultimate trust. May you and I never sleep on our watch. The armies of history have rewarded such treachery with a firing squad.

"But when the fullness of time was come, God sent forth his Son, made of a woman, made under the law, to redeem them that were under the law, that we might receive the adoption of sons" (Galatians 4:4-5).

Are You Crazy?

One of my preaching buddies, Scotty, and I braved a cold California Saturday, cold by Southern California's standards, that is, to preach in the open air at Huntington Beach. We had a heckler on the microphone, who was a science teacher and was a little contentious when it came to the gospel. The reason for the contention was that he had his own image of what God was like, and so the moral Law offended him. It rocked his idol. When he heard that God considered lust to be adultery, his reaction was to say, "What's wrong with lust? This is Huntington Beach, with all its pretty girls. Are you crazy?"

I said, "Hey, but that's like saying a little pedophilia is okay? It's pleasurable. Are you crazy?"

He looked at me and replied with a refreshing, "You have a point there." Wow.

He told us that someone had invited him to go to church the next day and that he was going to go. He then revealed another misconception about the gospel when he said, "God murdered His own Son? That makes no sense!" When I explained that God was in Christ, reconciling the world to himself, that Jesus of Nazareth was "the express image of the invisible God," that God became a man, and He was made manifest in the flesh, it was as if a light went on in his head.

During our discussion he said that we had destroyed everything he believed, but admitted afterwards that it had been an interesting time. That was very encouraging. Even though I froze to the bone, it is well worth it when God gives light to even one sinner who is sitting in the dark shadow of death.

"To wit, that God was in Christ, reconciling the world to himself, not imputing their trespasses to them; and has committed to us the word of reconciliation" (2 Corinthians 5:19).

EMPATHY HURTS

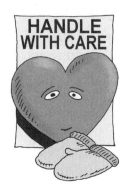

I've shed a lot of tears in recent years—from 9/11—over live pictures of people dying, starving children, and the world's daily pains. There have been times when I have wished that I wasn't so tender-hearted, but being a Christian means that we are touched with the feeling of other people's pains, distressing though it may be.

This includes knowledge of the unspeakable horror of eternal judgment. It means that we are sorrowful because we are acquainted with grief. The world can tune out, but we dare not. So never think of asking God to take away your tender heart, and never allow it to become calloused through apathy. It is compassion that warms our prayers and fires our zeal to reach the lost.

"And hope makes not ashamed; because the love of God is shed abroad in our hearts by the Holy Spirit which is given to us" (Romans 5:5).

DON'T FILL IN THE BLANKS

The following hot email was sent by an atheist to our ministry, and ended up on the desk of Mark Spence, the Dean of the School of Biblical Evangelism, around the middle of 2007:

"You're a real *blank* you degenerate scum ... so don't you ever *blank* tell me anything *blank* you're probably a *blank* child molester, you worthless coward ... don't give me your *blank blank* lies about best intentions ... you guys are just too *blank blank* self-centered to do anything and that is the fact I never hear anything Biblical come out of your filthy mouth, you brainwashed Nazi."

Instead of deleting the email, Mark responded kindly, and found that the man was upset because he was in pain, and couldn't afford medical treatment. We mentioned his dilemma in our monthly newsletter, and some of you kindly stepped up to the plate. Thank you. Here the man's latest email:

"What I wanted to tell you was thank you very much for doing what you did in spite of my insulting behavior. One very kind man ... paid for my MRI and a few doctor visits to get the reports done. Also another one of your readers made some donations for my medical bills, which was very Christian of him ... so thanks very much, you have made a difference in my life and so have those others who helped a complete stranger. It's unfortunate that only a small percentage of people who call themselves Christians actually act like it and have the actions to back up their words ... thanks, and take care.

"And be kind one to another, tenderhearted, forgiving one another, even as God for Christ's sake has forgiven you" (Ephesians 4:32).

Something Amazing

I was talking with a friend who regularly runs "The Way of the Master" evangelism classes. He said that when the class starts there is always a good turnout, but when people realize that they actually have to go out and speak to the lost, he loses about a third of them. He is grieved when it happens, even though he explains that through the class they would learn to share their faith without fear.

If those who deserted the battlefield had stayed, they would have found out something amazing. Imagine that you and I are standing beside a swimming pool in which there are large chunks of ice. I soberly say, "Two minutes in that freezing water and you will be dead! I dare you to jump in and do a length." You would no doubt have the good sense not to. However, if your two-year-old child fell in and began to drown, how long would you hesitate to dive in and save him? Not for a second. But wouldn't you be fearful of the freezing water? Of course not. Not for a second. That's the power of love.

So, do you hesitate to enter the freezing waters of evangelism to seek and save the lost? Do you listen to your fears? That's how to gauge the depth of your love.

"But you shall receive power, after that the Holy Spirit is come upon you: and you shall be witnesses to me both in Jerusalem, and in all Judea, and in Samaria, and to the uttermost part of the earth" (Acts 1:8).

WHY HE "SNAPPED"

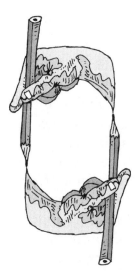

On December 8, 2008, the Omaha Police Department released a three-page suicide note left by Robert A. Hawkins, the twenty-year-old who fatally shot eight people at an Omaha shopping mall before turning the gun on himself. In the telling note, it's clear that Hawkins wasn't the loner he was first made out to be. He didn't lack friends. He said, "You guys are the best friends anyone could ever ask for." Rather, the note said exactly why he snapped. It said, "I've just snapped. I can't take this meaningless existence anymore ..."

If the secular world insists on saying that there is no God and that we are the products of evolutionary chance, they are saying that they have no idea where we came from, what we are doing here, or where we are going after death. Robert A. Hawkins is the tragic result of that meaningless existence.

"Let not mercy and truth forsake you: bind them about your neck; write them upon the table of your heart: so shall you find favor and good understanding in the sight of God and man" (Proverbs 3:3-4).

HOW DID HE KNOW?

I read recently where a number of evangelists gathered in Florida to discuss strategies for reaching the lost. It was said of one of them: "This humble man ... has led forty-seven million people to Christ." Does he have access to the Book of Life? How does he know that all of the forty-seven million were true converts? Doesn't he understand the biblical reality of true and false conversion?

The Bible tells us in Mark 4, and in other places, of spurious conversion, and it warns that the false convert will end up in a worse state than the first—like a pig that goes back to the filth. From what I understand, this evangelist doesn't use the Law to bring the knowledge of sin, so if statistics hold true, more than forty million of his converts have fallen away from the faith, and will have proven to be spurious. (See *The Way of the Master*, Bridge-Logos Publishers, for statistics). Such evangelism is an unspeakable tragedy, and is counterproductive to the Great Commission.

"And these are they by the way side, where the word is sown; but when they have heard, Satan comes immediately, and takes away the word that was sown in their hearts" (Mark 4:15).

A Certain Centurion

Before I became a Christian, I'm sure that most of my friends thought well of me. I was a fine and friendly young businessman. We tend to think well of our friends. This was the case in Luke chapter 7 when some people spoke of a certain centurion. They said that Jesus should heal this man's servant because the centurion was worthy (verse 4). He was a Roman and yet he loved the Jews, and he had even built them a synagogue. But the centurion knew better. When he heard that Jesus was coming to his house, he sent friends ahead to tell Him something he felt was of great importance. Listen to his words: *"I'm not worthy ..."* (verse 7). That's the only attitude in which any sinner can receive the Savior.

"Wherefore neither thought I myself worthy to come to you: but say in a word, and my servant shall be healed" (Luke 7:7).

Fat Baby

In China, a drained mother had more than her hands full. She had a hungry baby who was only eight months old and yet weighed an incredible forty-one pounds. That's huge. There was a reason for the extra weight. She breast-fed him twenty times a day! He was so fat that he couldn't even crawl. That's not good for a baby, but it's good for the Christian. We should daily desire the sincere milk of the Word, delight our souls in fatness, and then burn off the fat by reaching out to the lost.

"As newborn babes, desire the sincere milk of the word, that you may grow thereby" (1 Peter 2:2).

God Bless the Man

For two-and-a-half years, my son-in-law, EZ, and I preached open air almost every day outside the local courts. It was a wonderful opportunity to respectfully reach out to the lost. The area in which we spoke was public domain, and so free speech was our First Amendment right. That's what America is all about—the land of liberty, home of the brave, right? However, one local judge didn't like what we were doing, and so he changed the law and made the area court property, so we couldn't even step foot on it. Even our skillful lawyers couldn't fight that, so we thanked God for the times we had had there, and began open-air preaching at Huntington Beach each Saturday instead.

Yet, when I pass there each day, I can't help but grieve when I see lines of people waiting to enter the courts. But God is always in control. When Paul was imprisoned, he told the Philippians that what seemed negative was actually working out for the furtherance of the gospel. Christians were hearing about his arrest, and so they were stirred to open-air preach and to witness all over the place:

"But I want you to know, brethren, that the things which happened to me have actually turned out for the furtherance of the gospel, so that it has become evident to the whole palace guard, and to all the rest, that my chains are in Christ; and most of the brethren in the Lord, having become confident by my chains, are much more bold to speak the word without fear" (Philippians 1:12-14).

That's exactly what has happened in our case. Since the judge put our fire out, other fires have sprung up all over the country. Many people that are lined up outside of courthouses are now having the gospel of everlasting life preached to them, all because of this one anti-Christian judge. God bless him.

"Preach the word; be instant in season, out of season; reprove, rebuke, exhort with all longsuffering and doctrine" (2 Timothy 2:2).

Ignorant Biker

I once knew an elderly woman who was driven to despair, because she had a loud ringing in her ear, twenty-four-hours-a-day. A man once unwittingly started a motorbike in front of her and the noise was so loud, it burst her eardrum. He rode off not knowing the terrible damage he had caused to this poor woman.

The modern church is like that biker. It makes a big noise over its millions of decisions for Christ. But because they unwittingly use unbiblical methods, what they are doing is deafening sinners to the true gospel. The hardest people to witness to are the tragic products of modern evangelism, those we erroneously call backsliders.

"Having a form of godliness, but denying the power thereof: from such turn away" (2 Timothy 3:5).

Amazing!

Have you ever thought about the first recorded sermon that Jesus ever preached? In Luke 4:16, He told His hearers that God's favor isn't drawn out by anything in them; none of them deserved His blessings, or even His smile. How did they receive that first sermon? They tried to kill the preacher. In fact, those who heard Jesus preach tried to kill Him ten times before He even got to the Cross. The world may sing of the sweet sound of God's amazing grace, but their self-righteousness reveals that they see no need for it. We don't have a popular message, but the truth is that God's amazing grace is only for the lost, blind, and wicked wretches ... like me.

"And he said, Verily I say to you, No prophet is accepted in his own country" (Luke 4:24).

Another Gunman

Twenty-year-old Robert A. Hawkins got his wish. He became instantly famous. He is now known for murdering eight people, and then committing suicide at a mall in Nebraska. Once again, experts will profile the killer to try and figure what drove him to do it. Here's his profile: nice guy, friendly, not violent, funny, broke up with his girlfriend, was quiet until you got to know him, had bouts of depression, and had lost a job. He sounds like an average American with the usual problems that are faced by millions. So why did he go on a murderous rampage?

Here's the answer: He didn't fear God. Had he feared God, he wouldn't have hated another person, let alone killed nine people for no real reason. When life hurts and you want to lash out at this world, if you don't believe that you have to face a holy God, then why not do it? You are just glorified primal sludge with no purpose for existence. So why not go out with a bang, take a few with you, and at the same time become famous?

As Christians, we need to faithfully preach the fear of the Lord, and we can do that best by opening up the commandments as Jesus did. We must speak of Judgment Day; we must never hold back from preaching the reality of hell; and we must teach about a God who even sees our thought-lives. All this is from

the view of absolute holiness. That will drive sinners to the Cross, and that's where the sin that compels people to murder is dealt with in a heartbeat. There, at the foot of a bloodstained Cross, God gives us a heart that loves righteousness, and loves our neighbor as much as we love ourselves.

"Jesus said to him, You shall love the Lord your God with all your heart, and with all your soul, and with all your mind. This is the first and great commandment. And the second is like it, You shall love your neighbor as yourself" (Matthew 22:37-39).

ARIZONA ATHEIST

"Hmmm ..." says the Arizona Atheist. "Well, what if the Christian is wrong? What if Allah is the one true god? Then the Christian is in just as much trouble as the atheist. But since these imaginary people don't exist, no one has to worry about any of that anyway."

Dear Arizona Atheist, I don't believe you exist. I don't believe anyone wrote your comment. That may sound stupid, but that's what the professing atheist does. Let me explain by quoting from a new book I have called *How to Know God Exists:* "The DNA Factor."

"Think for a moment if you could ever believe that the book you are holding happened by accident. Here's the argument: There was nothing. Then paper appeared, and ink fell from nowhere onto the flat paper and shaped itself into perfectly formed letters of the English alphabet. Initially, the letters said something like this: "fgsn&k cn1clxc dumbh cckvkduh vstupidm ncncx."

As you can see, random letters rarely produce words that make sense. But in time, mindless chance formed them into the order of meaningful words with spaces between them. Periods, commas, capitals, italics, quotes, paragraphs, margins, etc., also came into being in the correct placements. The sentences then grouped themselves so that they related to each other, giving them coherence. Page numbers fell in sequence at the right places, and headers, footers, and footnotes appeared from nowhere on the pages, matching the portions of text to which they related. The paper trimmed itself and bound itself into a book. The ink for the cover fell from different directions, being careful not to incorrectly mingle with the other colors, forming itself into the graphics, title, and author's name.

There are multiple copies of this book, so the book then developed the ability to replicate itself thousands of times over. With this thought in mind, notice that in the following description of DNA, it is likened to a book:

"If you think of your genome (all of your chromosomes) as the book that makes you, then the genes are the words that make up the story . . . The letters that make up the words are called DNA bases, and there are only four of them: adenine (A), guanine (G), cytosine (C), and thymine (T). It's hard to believe that an alphabet with only four letters can make something as wonderful and complex as a person!"[1]

"To liken DNA to a book is a gross understatement. The amount of information in the three billion base pairs in the DNA in every human cell is equivalent to that in 1,000 books of encyclopedia size."[2] "It would take a person typing sixty words per minute, eight hours a day, for around fifty years to type the human genome. And if all the DNA in your body's one hundred trillion cells was put end to end, it would reach to the sun (ninety million miles away) and back over 600 times."[3]

[1] *Kids' Genetics*, GlaxoSmithKline http://genetics.gsk. com/kids/dna01.htm.
[2] Denton, *Evolution: Theory in Crisis.*
[3] "Genome Facts," Nova Online.

THE DIFFERENCE

Have you ever read about the church in the Book of Acts, and deliberately compared it to today's church and its agenda? There is a huge disparity. When the Holy Spirit was given on the Day of Pentecost, the disciples didn't stay for a further time of worship in the Upper Room—they immediately preached the gospel to the unsaved, as they had been told to do so. (See Mark 16:15.) Every corner they turned, they reached out to the lost.

Perhaps the difference between the modern church and the early church is that early believers were eternity-minded. That's what happens when someone comes to true repentance and faith in Jesus. He or she says, "Not my will, but Yours be done." The modern church lives for the present. It is concerned with itself and what it can get from God. You just have to watch Christian TV to see that. It is in essence saying, "Not Your will, but mine be done." So few are horrified at the fate of the lost. May God awaken the millions who sleep in such a spurious state within the Church.

"And he said to them, Go into all the world, and preach the gospel to every creature" (Mark 16:15).

DOG AND PONY SHOW

"Ray," one brother writes, "I don't believe dog-and-pony shows should be mixed with the gospel. 'Vain jesting' and the like derides the solemnity and seriousness of the state the lost are in ... Light shows, magic tricks and comedy acts have no place with the gospel."

I'm not sure of this brother's past experiences. Perhaps he has seen some horrible pulpit humor or some distasteful youth-group pranks mixed in with the message. But I have to make a defense, so that others won't be discouraged from legitimate and biblical ways to reach the lost.

This brother's words were probably in response to my using sleight-of-hand to relate to six young people. Or maybe it was in response to something I did earlier, which was blowing up a latex glove and then bursting it to illustrate how our lives are like a vapor that vanishes in an instant. Is such a thing a dog-and-pony show, or is it biblical?

Throughout the Old Testament, the prophets of God would take clay vessels and smash them, or use wineskins and other objects to enforce their words. Jesus asked for a coin to make a point. He could have merely said that Caesar's inscription was on the coin, but He had one brought to Him. People are more likely to remember something if they see it with the eye, as well as hear it with the ear.

I also think that it's biblical to begin a gospel message in the natural realm. Nathan spoke of a lamb when he addressed David. Jesus spoke of water with the woman at the well, and Paul quoted secular poets as he preached open air on Mars Hill. Lambs, water, and poetry were used as springboards for the message, but some of the things we do in the natural realm have nothing to do with the message. They are merely ways in which we attract a crowd. Once they gather, then we swing to the subject of the things of God. One way we often do this is to ask the crowd trivia questions, and give prizes to those who get a right answer and "Giant Money" tracts to those who get the answer wrong. The gifts create good will among the hearers and make it easier for them to listen to us. Some may not like to do this, but we do because we like it when 100 to150 people gather and then stay for an hour-and-a-half and listen to the gospel.

I have a dear friend who is extremely funny, and is part of "Clean Comedians." He makes people laugh. Once they feel comfortable, he then presents the Law and the blood of the Cross. Humor was something strongly encouraged by Charles Spurgeon who said, "I sometimes tickle my oyster until he opens his shell, and then I slip the knife in."

So never be discouraged from being innovative and making sinners smile. Follow the example of a good doctor who takes a moment to make his patient feel comfortable, before he gives him a sobering diagnosis, and then presents the cure. Other doctors may criticize him for such trifling ... but he knows that he does it because he deeply cares about his patient.

> *"To the weak became I as weak, that I might gain the weak: I am made all things to all men, that I might by all means save some. And this I do for the gospel's sake"* (1 Corinthians 9:22-23).

POTENTIAL MOVIE

In September of 2007, we filmed a program for our TV show called "What Scares You?" The opening scene was a cowboy shootout between Kirk Cameron and myself. I was so excited by the quality of production that I immediately wrote a script for a full-length, period-piece Western. Too many Christian  films have a soft message or allegories that are hidden from the unsaved. This one weaves the biblical gospel into a very exciting plot, in a way that has never been done before.

> *"Therefore, my beloved brethren, be steadfast, unmoveable, always abounding in the work of the Lord, forasmuch as you know that your labor is not in vain in the Lord"* (1 Corinthians 15:58).

Get Him!

I am going through all sixty-three tapes of European footage for the fourth season of our television show. My job is to log what works and what doesn't, before it goes to the editor. It is laborious, but at the same time there's some exciting video. I was open-air preaching in the early hours of the morning in Brussels to a booze-drinking crowd when someone called out that I should be more tolerant. I had said that Jesus was the only way to God. A few minutes later things got slightly tense between myself and another heckler. Suddenly, Mr. Tolerant called to the crowd, "Get him! Get him!" That stirred them into a frenzied lynch mob. Fortunately for me, the first heckler I was speaking to screamed, "Stop it! Stop this!" and the crowd backed off. So much for tolerance.

"Jesus said to him, I am the way, the truth, and the life: no man comes to the Father, but by me" (John 14:6).

Never Hesitate

Sadly, we had to have our dog put down recently. As Sue and I were leaving the veterinarian's office, we noticed that a mother and her grown daughter were sobbing deeply, because they had just put their dog down. Suddenly I had a big dilemma. Sue was in tears; they were in tears. Do I or don't I offer these grieving people

a "Million Dollar Bill" tract? How could I? How insensitive! I decided to do it despite my fears.

I opened the door for them and said, "We just lost our dog too. Here's something to cheer you up. It's a million dollars." I was amazed to see that both women immediately burst into laughter. I quickly added, "You will probably need it to pay the vet bill." They laughed again. They were still smiling as they walked down the sidewalk. Perhaps we should do hospital drops. If we ever get another dog, I think I will name it "Stay." It would be interesting to see what he will do when I call "Come here, Stay!"

> *"Blessed be God, even the Father of our Lord Jesus Christ, the Father of mercies, and the God of all comfort; who comforts us in all our tribulation, that we may be able to comfort them which are in any trouble, by the comfort wherewith we ourselves are comforted of God"* (2 Corinthians 1:3-4).

How to Dissipate Pulpit Fears

One major fear most preachers have is of standing in a pulpit and somehow messing up and looking foolish in front of a crowd of people. I have used a strategy for years that can help with such fears. If something goes wrong, I simply say, "Turn to Exodus 20:11, put your finger there and then turn over to 1 Timothy 1:9."  That gives me at least thirty seconds to pull my thoughts together or to find my place in my notes.

I then say, "I have no idea what those verses are. I just wanted to give you something to do while I found my place in my notes." That makes people laugh and at the same time relieves any tension in the air. Just knowing that you have that option can help you conquer your fears.

"Fear not, little flock; for it is your Father's good pleasure to give you the kingdom" (Luke 12:32).

You Can Do It

It was a freezing day by Southern California standards, and the area where we normally preached was like a desert, so I decided to give out some "Giant Money" tracts and perhaps do some one-to-one witnessing. I was reminded of how easy it is to give out those giant $100 bills. People loved them, and a number came up and actually asked for them. The tracts are so big that when people walked off holding them, they acted as their own advertisement and others then wanted them.

I saw six teenagers sitting on the ground. They loved the tracts, so I asked, "Do you like magic?" They did. So I turned two one-dollar bills into a five-dollar bill. They loved that more than they loved the tracts, so I asked what they thought happened when someone dies. That opened the doors to a wonderful time of sharing the gospel.

Perhaps you are thinking that you could never do magic. Yes, you can. It's easy after a little practice and the advantages are enormous for breaking the ice with strangers. You can learn how to turn two ones into a five by going to http://www.livingwaters.com/m_equip.shtml Scroll down to "Create your own money trick."

"For I am not ashamed of the gospel of Christ: for it is the power of God to salvation to every one that believes; to the Jew first, and also to the Greek" (Romans 1:16).

The Power of Humor

Someone wrote to me recently and asked how they could best present the subject of biblical evangelism to a group at their church. I said that one of most effective ways to hold the attention of your hearers is to use a little humor here and there. It's like a flash of lightning during a dark night. It wakes people up and they tend to wait for the next one. I told him that if he wasn't the humorous type, to read a couple of one-liners from "The World's Best One-liners" tract. He did, and said that it went very well.

"The joy of the Lord is your strength" (Nehemiah 8:10).

What Would You Do?

Here are three thought-provoking questions you might ask when witnessing. I have used these on "The Way of the Master" radio program and for the third season of our television program, and they elicit interesting answers:

1. It's 1938. You have been taken back in time. You have Adolph Hitler in the sights of a high-powered rifle. He was later to be responsible for the deaths of millions of Jews, Gypsies, blacks, and homosexuals. Over sixty million people died because of the war that he started. One squeeze of the trigger, you take him out, and save all those lives. Do you pull the trigger? Most, without hesitation, say they would. Okay. It's forty years earlier. You have Adolph Hitler's mother in the sights of that same rifle. She's pregnant with Adolph. Do you take her out? Most say they wouldn't. Then you ask

why? Does God have anything to do with the answer?

2. A massive asteroid is going to hit the Earth and destroy it in one hour. What would you do for those sixty minutes?

3. You are to be banished to an island by yourself. You are allowed one book. What would it be? Would you consider the Bible? Why? Why not?

"But seek first the kingdom of God, and his righteousness; and all these things shall be added to you" (Matthew 6:33).

A Cause for Concern

I noticed that crowds of Muslims waved their arms and wielded machetes, because they were incensed that an English schoolteacher gave permission for a seven-year-old child to name his teddy bear "Mohammed."

It made me think of an atheist friend who has a false name. This is because he fears that Christians may try to kill him because of his atheist convictions. I dropped him a friendly note and said that he shouldn't have any concerns about Christians. We love him.

However, he should be concerned that all over the Internet are video clips of him and his buddies blaspheming God, and saying, "I am not afraid." I said that if Arab TV ever runs a news story about hundreds of Americans who are blaspheming God's name and saying that they are not afraid, they will broadcast the item in the Arabic language ... and Arabic for God is "Allah." That's a real reason for concern.

"There is no fear in love; but perfect love casts out fear: because fear has torment. He that fears is not made perfect in love" (1 John 4:18).

Ready for the Secret Service

The "Million Dollar Bill" tract not only made the Home Page of Foxnews.com recently, but it was also on Yahoo's Home Page and in *USA Today*. While this is wonderful publicity, I'm wondering if the Secret Service isn't going to arrest me for being the bill's creator. So I have a solid defense ready. I will tell the judge that the tract evolved. There was nothing. Then there was a huge bang, and paper formed. Ink then fell onto the paper, and through a series of amazing mutations, a one-dollar bill was formed. As millions of years passed, it then formed itself into the "Million Dollar Bill" tract, and that it reproduced itself. So, I am guiltless. With today's court system and with so many people naively believing in the theory-tale of evolution, I would probably get away with it.

"And we know that we are of God, and the whole world lies in wickedness" (1 John 5:19).

Here We Go Again

Someone tried to bank another one of our "Million Dollar Bill" tracts. Fortunately, the bank teller was highly trained, and even though the tract was crumpled up to disguise itself, he thought that the transaction was suspicious and called the police.

Here's the item: "AIKEN, SC (WIS)— Authorities say a bank teller in Clearwater had a million reasons not to open an account for an Augusta, Georgia, man. Aiken County Sheriff's spokesman Lieutenant Michael Frank says 31-year-old Alexander D. Smith tried to open an account Monday with a fake $1 million bill. Franks says the employee refused to open the account and called police while the man started to curse at bank workers. Frank says Smith has been charged with disorderly conduct and two counts of forgery. Authorities say the federal government has never printed a million-dollar bill."

"No man can serve two masters: for either he will hate the one, and love the other; or else he will hold to the one, and despise the other. You cannot serve God and mammon" (Matthew 6:24).

I'M PRETTY SHALLOW

I was visiting a friend's church, and just after sitting down I sent him a quick text message to let him know I was there. A few minutes later, during the meet-and-greet time, an elderly lady next to me said, "You shouldn't be playing games in church. It's irreverent!" I felt terrible, and politely said, "Oh, it's not a game. I was sending a text mes ..." She interrupted, "That doesn't matter!" and walked off.

Suddenly I had a big problem. Instead of enjoying church, I found myself reacting like a five-year-old kid. I wanted to send more text messages, and then stick my tongue out at her as I sent them. When she whispered to her husband during the sermon, I had to stop myself from tapping her on the arm and saying, "Shhhh! That's irreverent." When she left before the close of the service, I wanted to run after her and tell her how rude she was to leave before the end. Of course, I asked God to forgive me for such thoughts.

I have often thought of what I would have done if I were Jesus after He rose from the dead. I would have immediately gone to see the High Priest and the Sanhedrin. I would have knocked on the door and before they opened it, I would have stepped through it and said, "Hey, how are you doing? Remember me? Huh? Huh?" I'm pretty shallow. But Jesus didn't do that. God is a God of grace, so perhaps some of those men were there at Pentecost, repenting for their murderous deed.

"Forgive, and you shall be forgiven" (Luke 6:37).

Fun Lesson for Kids

We had our family with us for Thanksgiving. My daughter was a little nervous because she had plans to give a Bible lesson to the grandchildren, and she wondered if trying to work with very young children would be a disaster. Perhaps she remembered the time I gave our three kids their first communion,  during family devotions. The two youngest got into a fight about who had the most grape juice. It was a disaster. Despite her fears, it turned out great.

My son-in-law blindfolded each of the kids and spoke to them about being thankful to God for eyesight. He then put a little bit of tape over their mouths and talked about being thankful for the ability to speak. He put their hands behind their backs and had them eat a cookie from a plate on the floor, and talked about how wonderful it is to have hands. It was a lot of fun for the kids, and it was a good reminder for them, and for us adults, of how much we take for granted.

"In every thing give thanks: for this is the will of God in Christ Jesus concerning you" (1 Thessalonians 5:18).

Birthdays and Birds

To my amazement, I am now fifty-eight years old. I say "amazement" because life has gone by so quickly. For years, I would gently say to any elderly men who cut me off while driving, "Hey, watch it, grandpa!" I have stopped saying that now that I have seven grandchildren. If you are worried about getting old, or you want to console someone who is, there is one really positive thing about aging. No, it's not senor discounts. It's actually getting old.

Think about how many millions didn't get to do that. They died in their youth. Think of the twenty million people who died in the First World War. Most of them were soldiers who were in the prime of life, probably in their twenties. Or think of the sixty-one million whose lives were taken in the Second World War. Then think of all the other wars in history, all the young people who have been taken by disease, or killed by cars, and as a result of other accidents.

I remember when I was sixteen-years-old and was pulled under the water while surfing. I became disoriented and mistakenly swam towards the bottom instead of towards the surface. When I did break through and gasped for air, I almost sucked in a passing seagull. I was surfing alone. It was getting dark. I could have easily drowned. But I didn't, and now more than forty years later, I'm still alive and kicking.

So gratitude for life itself has helped me have a positive attitude towards something that is depressing for most. Compared to the fate of millions of others, I am incredibly blessed. Add to that the fact that I have everlasting life in Christ, and I am unspeakably blessed beyond words.

Open-air Preaching

One new way we have been getting peoples' attention when we preach is to have someone blow up a latex glove until it's about two feet in diameter and then twist the end. While the person is blowing up the glove into a large balloon, we ask the gathering crowd to name famous people from the past who have died. People call out, "Shakespeare, Napoleon, John Wayne, Marilyn Monroe," etc. Then I say, "The Bible says, '… for what is your life? It is even a vapor, that appears for a little time, and then vanishes away'" (James 4:14). When I say, "vanish," I stick a pin in the balloon and it goes off with a huge bang. Then I say, "The second you die, no matter who you are, how famous you are, or what you have achieved, it's all going to mean nothing on that day. So please listen carefully to what I'm going to tell you about why we die, and what we can do about it."

It's very visual, gathers a crowd, makes a good point, and goes off with a bang. Another way you can do this is by saying that many people believe that they are going to Heaven because they are good and do good things. Then relate it to a criminal admitting to the judge that he's guilty of a murderous crime, but he also says, "I'm a good person and I do good things." Then say, "When you stand before God with all your good works, they are going to mean this much …," then stick the pin in the balloon. The only way to be saved is to trust in God's mercy. In the words of the old hymn, "Nothing in my hand I bring. Simply to Thy Cross I cling." Or you can use the four fingers and the thumb that stick out of the top of the balloon to go through five of the Commandments.

"Whereas you know not what shall be on the morrow. For what is your life? It is even a vapor, that appears for a little time, and then vanishes away" (James 4:14).

Bird-brain Thoughts

Apparently, the most common bird is the sparrow, whose life span is twenty-three years. Jesus spoke of how God takes care of the lowly sparrow and how He will take care of you and me because we are of more value than they. But have you ever wondered why we don't see aging sparrows? Every one I see seems to be young, happy, and healthy. They are not slow moving, arthritic, and elderly. Or is there a convalescent tree somewhere for elderly sparrows that are waiting to die?

And, if there are as many as 400 billion birds, as the experts tell us, and each dies after twenty or so years, why don't we see dead birds everywhere? While I am on the subject of birds, why don't they interbreed? Dogs can be interbred. So can cats and horses, but we don't see that happen with birds. I have yet to hear of an owl mating with an eagle (an eagowl) or a parrot and a sparrow (a sparrot).

"Fear not therefore, you are of more value than many sparrows" (Matthew 10:31).

THE PERFECT CRIME

Hollywood is fascinated when someone gets away with murder. They call it the perfect crime. But perfect murders are not "few and far between." Between 1951 and 2007, there were 851,063 murders in the United States [1]. During that time there were 296,000 "perfect crimes" [2]. That's how many unsolved homicides there were during that time.

Bringing that figure up in preaching and witnessing is a powerful way to reason with the unsaved about the reality of hell. If a judge is good, he must strive to see that justice is done--that murderers are punished. Any judge who turns a blind eye to murder is extremely corrupt, and should be charged with a crime himself. Most people will acknowledge that God is good, and if He is good He must bring every one of those murderers to justice. If He doesn't, He is corrupt by nature.

However, God is so good He will "bring every work to justice, including every secret thing." (See Ecclesiastes 12:14.) He also punishes rapists, thieves, liars, adulterers, blasphemers, and fornicators. He will even judge down to the thoughts and intents of the human heart. He considers lust to be adultery, and hatred, murder … and the prison to which He will send them forever is called hell.

[1] www.ojp.usdoj.gov/bjs/homicide/tables/totalstab.htm
[2] www.unknownnews.net/030908csi.html

"For God shall bring every work into judgment, with every secret thing, whether it be good, or whether it be evil" (Ecclesiastes 12:14).

THE CHASE

I am still regularly being chased by a livid Chihuahua. The other morning when I heard him running down his driveway, I steered my bike across the street. When he chased me, I stopped and said a sweet, "Hi ya, fellow." (His owner was watching.) He backed up (the dog, that is), and when I took off, he chased me down the street again. On my way home that evening, he came out of his driveway like a flaming cannonball. I couldn't figure how he could growl and run so fast at the same time. He was so intent on getting me I thought he had misjudged his speed and was going to end up in the spokes of my front wheel. The image of a Chihuahua in a blender made me scream out loud. This is getting weird.

"The Lord is my light and my salvation; whom shall I fear? The Lord is the strength of my life; of whom shall I be afraid" (Psalm 27:1).

My Dumb Thoughts

For years I have wondered why we throw away banana peels. Their only purpose seems to be something to slip on, as in some slapstick comedy. But I have always noticed that we eat apple skins, orange peels, peach, and apricot skins. My thought is that surely God has a reason for such a thick wrapper on the banana. I would often say that it might contain something medically wonderful.

I felt vindicated recently when some kind person sent me this news item: "Researchers have discovered that banana peel extract can ease depression and protect the retina, a Chinese-language newspaper said yesterday. Researchers from Chung Shan Medical University in Taichung, after two years of research, have discovered that banana peel is rich in serotonin, which is vital to balancing moods," the *Apple Daily* reported. "The research team said it believes  consuming banana peel by boiling the peel and drinking the water or by putting it through a fruit juicer and drinking the juice can help ease depression. It suggested drinking banana peel water or juice every evening or several times a week." Maybe the Chinese could produce a toy that has been soaked in banana extract, that depressed and near-sighted kids could chew on.

"To every thing there is a season, and a time to every purpose under the heaven" (Ecclesiastes 3:1).

DON'T TELL ANYONE THIS ...

Never tell me a secret. I'm serious. I can't stand knowing something, especially when it's good news. When our kids were little, much to Sue's dismay, I would get up early on Christmas morning and stomp up and down the hallway until they woke up. I couldn't wait to give them their gifts. By the way; if you haven't heard of a teaching called "Hell's Best Kept Secret," I have something exciting I want to tell you ... (www.livingwaters. com/learn/hellsbestkeptsecret.htm)

"The lips of the wise disperse knowledge" (Proverbs 15:7).

CRAZY WORLD

By mid-November 2007, nearly 4,000 U.S. soldiers had tragically died in the Iraq War. That's 4,000 precious human beings—somebody's loving brother or sister, or beloved son or daughter. Gone. Forever. On the same date CBS reported that 200,000 people die each year in the U.S. because of medical mistakes. Then the news reader casually moved on to another story. What? *Two hundred thousand people!* That's 200,000 human beings—someone's loving brother or sister, or beloved son or daughter, mother or father. Gone. Forever. Who needs enemies when you have a friendly medical profession

that accidentally kills the equivalent of three full Super Bowl stadiums each year?

> *"The sting of death is sin; and the strength of sin is the law"* (1 Corinthians 15:56).

ATHEISM

Athiesm   Religion

Few would deny that there's a rising tide of atheism in America and throughout the world. Three books on the subject were on the "New York Times" best-seller list at the same time. The common denominator with the authors is that they have a deep contempt for religion--and so they should, with so many money-hungry evangelists, hypocritical churchgoers, and pedophile priests.

Religion is the second largest cause of suffering and death throughout history. But atheistic communism comes in at number one, murdering over one-hundred million people to further its secular agenda.* What many fail to see is that it's not religion or communism that is the cause of so much human suffering and of so many deaths, but mankind, itself. There is something inherently wrong with man, evidenced, not only in his hatred and murder of his own kind, but also in his hatred and contempt for the God who gave him life. He will even go to the insane extreme of denying His existence—something as evident as the sun at noon on a cloudless day.

*Blurb from a new book, *How to Know God Exists* (published by Bridge-Logos Publishers).

> *"The heart is deceitful above all things, and desperately wicked: who can know it?"* (Jeremiah 17:9).

DEATHS IN AMERICA

Charles Spurgeon said that people could be taught to live by being reminded that they have to die. That's true. Sane human beings have a will to live, and it's an often-forgotten tool by which we may reason with them. So, here are some feathers for your evangelistic arrows:

Every year around 90,000 people die in hospitals from medical mistakes. That is one American who dies in a hospital from a medical error every six minutes. Medical blunders are the eighth leading cause of death in the United States. A horrifying 43,443 people died in car accidents in one year. That's one American killed in a traffic accident every twelve minutes. That may make you want to stay home. Think again. One American is killed in an accident at home every twenty-nine minutes for an annual total of over 18,000 deaths. One American is accidentally fatally poisoned every twenty-seven minutes for an annual total of 19,457. Falls killed 17,227 people back in 2004. That's one every thirty-one minutes. One American is killed by a drunk driver every thirty-one minutes, for a total of 16,885 per year. Murders are down since the 1990's, unless Hollywood has succeeded in teaching more people how to disguise them. One American is murdered every thirty-two minutes. According to the FBI, 17,034 people were murdered in 2006.

Sources:
National Safety Council, for 2006
National Vital Statistics Report, for 2006
Home Safety Council, for 2004
Mothers Against Drunk Driving, for 2005
Department of Justice, for 2004

One more to cheer you up: Every thirty seconds, a woman somewhere in the world gives birth to a child. She must be found and stopped.

"What man is he that lives, and shall not see death? Shall he deliver his soul from the hand of the grave?" (Psalm 89:48).

A Personal Note

I am consoled to know that Jesus was said to have an oil of joy above His fellows, and yet He was a man of sorrows, acquainted with grief. I'm sure you sometimes feel you could burst with joy when you think both of the greatness of God and what He did for us on the Cross.  We have great joy. But at the same time we are acquainted with grief. There is so much pain.

We are putting together a video for YouTube that addresses this subject: Why the increase of grief, particularly in America in the area of disease and suffering? It's called *The Divine Butler*. Please pray that God gives us wisdom. Also pray for our regular Saturday open-air preaching at Huntington Beach. Thanks for being part of this ministry.

"He is despised and rejected of men; a man of sorrows, and acquainted with grief: and we hid as it were our faces from him; he was despised, and we esteemed him not" (Isaiah 53:3).

WHICH CAME FIRST?

Sue and I have a chicken coop at home. I like chickens and even gave the ladies their own names. There's Fingerlickin', Roast, and Crispy, just to name a few. I put their names on the wall of the coop to remind them that they are to lay eggs for our family. It seems to be working.

So which came first, the chicken or the egg? In our case, it was the chicken and the first egg came some time later. However, it's not so simple among the Genesis-less generation [1]. Did the first chicken come from the first egg, or was it the chicken that first laid the first egg? Long ago, even Aristotle (384-322 BC) spoke of the egg dilemma. He philosophized: "For there could not have been a first egg to give a beginning to birds, or there should have been a first bird which gave a beginning to eggs; for a bird comes from an egg."

Let's get into a little philosophical talk ourselves. Let's say evolution was responsible for the beginning, and let's say the egg was the first to evolve, before the chicken. Why did it do that? Why would there be nothing, and over millions of years, nothing became simple organisms, and then these organisms became an egg? I can understand that a fish evolved legs and lungs over millions of years, because he and his necessary female helpmate wanted to breathe and to walk on dry land. But why would a thoughtless egg appear first and then want to become a chicken? How and why did it evolve with a yolk, a white, and a shell shaped like—like an egg? If the egg was shaped with a rounded point at each end for ease of laying (since a square egg would be painful) how did evolution know to make it that shape if there were never any chickens in the first place to know that an egg is made to be laid?

Another small dilemma: how did the first egg get fertilized to become the first chicken? What or who fertilized it, and why did he fertilize it and sit on it until it hatched? How did the fertilizing creature evolve and have the ability to fertilize an egg that he found? How did he get the seed into the egg to fertilize it? And why did the rooster evolve as a bird? Unless he was an egg first, and if so, we have the above questions to deal with, because his egg would also need to be fertilized. Who did the fertilizing?

Actually, we don't need to think at all. Evolutionists have it all worked out: "Chickens evolved from non-chickens through small changes caused by the mixing of male and female DNA or by mutations to the DNA that produced the zygote. These changes and mutations only have an effect at the point where a new zygote is created. That is, two non-chickens mated and the DNA in their new zygote contained the mutation(s) that produced the first true chicken. That one zygote cell divided to produce the first true chicken. Prior to that first true chicken zygote, there were only non-chickens. The zygote cell is the only place where DNA mutations could produce a new animal, and the zygote cell is housed in the chicken's egg. So, the egg must have come first." (www.howstuffworks.com/question85.htm)

"He that answers a matter before he hears it, it is folly and shame unto him" (Proverbs 18:13).

Next to Godliness

I was riding my bike to work and saw a puddle in front of me. My clothes were clean, and not wanting to get spots of water all over them, I rode onto the grass beside the puddle.

A friend at work kindly scraped all the mud off my back.

"Bear one another's burdens, and so fulfil the law of Christ" (Galatians 6:2).

Road Rage

Recently a dentist in New York found a car blocking his way into a parking lot. He became very angry and assaulted the driver, then a CBS cameraman who recorded the incident, and then he assaulted the driver's sister. CBS interviewed a

psychologist about the incident, and it turned out that the man had an "Impulse Control Disorder"—ICD. How about "Severe Internal Nastiness"—SIN?

"For all have sinned, and come short of the glory of God" (Romans 3:23).

Escape Artist

When we were in Europe filming the third season for our TV program, we had a member of our team escape from a straight jacket while wearing chains. It was a great way to illustrate that we are chained to death and hell by our sins.

Recently a genuine escape artist wrote to me and offered his services. He loves the Lord and is brilliant. He can get out of three sets of handcuffs in seconds. He appeared on an ABC television special, jumping from a plane while handcuffed. We are considering using him for our fifth season, due to be filmed late in 2008.

He gave a couple of interesting scenarios, so I wrote back with one of mine: "What if we put you into a straight jacket, chained, handcuffed, bound, hooded, gagged, soaked in gasoline, set on fire, thrown from a plane at 10,000 feet into a pit filled with viscious crocodiles, poisonous snakes, scorpions, spiders, sharks, fire ants, killer bees, and lawyers? From there you preach."

He replied, "Drop the lawyers and I'll do it."

"Nay, in all these things we are more than conquerors through him that loved us" (Romans 8:37).

How to Make an Eye

Recently, during open-air preaching, I heard a professing atheist boast that he could create a camera lens that worked better than the human eye. His inference was that God had botched it when He made the eye. I asked him how he

would create a camera lens from nothing. To truly create it, he couldn't use God's materials. He had to start from scratch. It seems he hadn't thought about that minor detail.

Yet, the most intelligent of us can't create anything from nothing. Only a simpleton would think he could. But the atheist goes one step further than a simpleton. He believes that in the beginning, no one made *everything* from *nothing.* No wonder the Bible calls him a fool (see Psalm 14:1).

"The fool has said in his heart, There is no God. They are corrupt, they have done abominable works, there is none that does good" (Psalm 14:1).

Mafia Standards

The Associated Press reported that the Italian police found a list of Ten Commandments for top Mafia bosses. The "Godfather's Ten Commandments" barred any hanging out in bars, befriending the police, being late for appointments, and looking at their friends' wives. Although it spoke of respecting one's wife, the Mafia must come first. Each member must be available at a moment's notice, "even if your wife is about to give birth." The final blurb set the standard for being in the Mob. Those who have no moral values cannot join. I'm speechless.

"There is no fear of God before their eyes" (Romans 3:18).

SHAKEN BACON

Since "The Way of the Master" radio program is broadcast to 200 radio stations in Australia, every couple of months we are obligated to do "phone fishing" with Aussies. I say obligated because I didn't like doing eight fifteen-minute sessions in a row. In the past I had found it mentally exhausting. Before we started I complained, moaned, and whined. I didn't want to do it. By the time we got to the fifth session, I had had enough.

I spoke to a twenty-two-year-old Aussie named Bret. Our contact informed us that he was covered in tattoos, with a pentagram on his hand. We talked about tattoos for a while, found out that he believed in Heaven, but didn't believe in hell. I took him through the Ten Commandments, then into grace, and talked about the reasonableness of hell, in the light of God being good and, therefore, just.

Then I said, "Does that make sense?"

He answered, "That is a complete load of sense. I'm thinking right now about getting a Bible."

I was speechless. I quickly passed the interview over to Todd, who said, "I'm begging you, get right with God."

Bret said, "You don't have to beg; I will. I'm sitting here shaking. I'm trembling." We commended him to our Aussie contact, who made sure he was given literature. What an encouragement! I'm looking forward to the next time we go down under.

"But as many as received him, to them gave he power to become the sons of God, even to them that believe on his name" (John 1:12).

Yipping Chihuahuas and a 90-Mile-an-Hour Cereal Box

Years ago, for some reason, I let a book which was a wonderful evangelistic tool, go out of print. It was about dumb things people have done, most of it being about my daily life. Fortunately, a publisher has decided to release it, and it will come out under a new title, *101 of the Dumbest Things People Have Done (published by Bridge-Logos Publishers, 2008).*

Most days I manage to do something really dumb, so I think we will end up with more than one volume. Just the other day I was riding to work on my bike, when I looked ahead and saw an angry and barking Chihuahua running toward me. The beast had chased me before, but never with a frontal attack. I didn't like the messy thought of having a head-on collision with a Chihuahua, so I crossed the street. He followed me, obviously encouraged by the fact that I didn't want to face him head-on. When I reached the opposite sidewalk, he backed off, still barking abuse. I spun a wheelie and yelled, "Hey, what's your problem!" That's when I noticed the dog's owner standing on his lawn, staring at me like I was some kind of nut. Suddenly a member of my staff drove by. She had seen the whole incident, slowed down, wound down her window, and with a big smile on her face she said, "Naughty doggy!" while waving her finger at me. I wasn't sure if she was speaking to the dog or me.

The next day I poured some cereal into a bowl, and was left holding an empty box. I decided that it would take up less room in the trash if I flattened it. So I put it on the floor, and stood on it. That's when I found out that a cereal box on a vinyl floor moves a person like he's on smooth ice. My foot slid at ninety-miles-an-hour into the dog dish and spread dog food and water all over the kitchen floor. I spent some quality time getting the food out of my shoe.

Earlier that week, I phoned my editor to wish her a happy birthday. I knew it was coming up so I kept a note all week by my phone that said, "Sunday: Birthday—Lynn." I even programmed my phone to sound an alarm. A birthday call out of the blue can be so meaningful. The Sunday came. I didn't lose the note. The alarm went off as planned. I felt proud of myself, and as I called I was thinking, "This will be a surprise." When she answered I blurted out a sincere and enthusiastic, "Happy birthday, Lynn!" Her birthday was the previous Sunday!

So if you too are a continual klutz, take comfort that you are not alone. There's a whole book coming to console you.

"... he that is of a merry heart has a continual feast" (Proverbs 15:15).

Police Shootout

The police had their guns drawn and aimed at Kirk and me as we lay in the dirt. I could hardly believe what was happening. Just seconds earlier we had been standing on a sidewalk, when two police cars sped toward us with their sirens blaring. We ran down the sidewalk, threw a bag of money into the trunk of our car, and like two terrified gazelles, ran into an open park. That's when we heard instructions to hit the dirt and toss our guns.

As I lay on my face, I listened to my loud breathing. The ski mask I was wearing was hindering my intake, and I was gasping for each breath. I wanted to rip the mask off but I didn't dare move my hands.

Suddenly Kirk cried out in terrible pain. At first I thought, "Now, that's good acting!" But I realized that he wasn't acting. I started to turn my head to the right to see if he was okay, and heard an officer scream at me to keep looking to the left. Someone approached me and I was handcuffed. My right cuff was so tight I moaned in pain. As I was turned over, I yelled as loud as Kirk did. I felt as though my shoulder was going to break.

A month earlier I had been held by Italian police for over an hour. That was real life. This was fake. But being held by the Italian police was nothing compared to this. As we sat, covered in dirt, handcuffed, and cramped in the squad car, I turned to Kirk and said, "Whose idea was this?"

He said, "*Yours!*"

The rest of the day's shoot hadn't been so painful. We had spent most of it in a prison cell, filming a program called, "Caught in a Lie." The program opens with the police chase, and shows us being handcuffed, thrust into the police car, and brought into custody. Duane Barnhart, our director/producer, told us earlier in the day that we'd been too passive in the first take, while being fingerprinted. He wanted to film it again, this time with a little resistance on our part.

At the beginning of the fingerprint process, I began the resistance. I was slow to put my left hand on my head when I was told to. When the officer said to move faster, I cleverly said, "Punk!" That got me a firm push against the wall with instructions to shut up and do exactly what I was told to do. I was on a roll. Somehow resistance was coming naturally.

Duane gestured to me that he wanted more. I had another brainstorm. As a very large officer moved my thumb in one direction, I cleverly resisted. So, how would he handle that?

Wham! I was suddenly slammed to my knees with my face on the concrete floor. On my violent and speedy way down, my head smashed into Kirk's knee as he sat handcuffed, watching the proceedings. I felt his pain because he was still reeling from the agony of having the same 260-pound officer's knee in his back so hard that he thought his spine was going to break.

I was on my knees, my face on the floor, my head was hurting, and my wrists were red and burning with pain. The big officer spat out, "Do you like being in this position?" Good sense told me to hold back from saying, "Hey, I'm a Christian. I'm on my knees. Of course I like this position."

After our mug shots were taken, we were marched, still in handcuffs, to a holding room, where we were put against the wall, searched, un-cuffed, and told to empty our pockets. We were then given orange uniforms. Although mine was a little loose, and the top didn't exactly match the bottom, I felt it was better not to mention it to the nice officer.

We were then put into an eight-by-six cell. The heavy iron door was slammed shut, and from there we spoke about how multitudes were arrested each year, and how many tried to outwit the long arm of the law.

Kirk then tried to outwit the long arm of a lie detector. We fed his examiner some information that gave Kirk something to lose if he failed. This was because the only way the polygraph machine would work, was for him to have something that would make him sweat if he lost. I knew of something that would make Kirk sweat a lot.

There was a natural tension during the test. We watched a monitor from another room, as we waited the long twenty-five seconds between ten questions. When the examiner revealed the results, something amazing happened that none of us were expecting, not even the examiner. It was a day we would never forget.

But something else happened at the conclusion of the shoot that, for me, seemed to solidify the whole experience.

As we were about to leave the station, a man was brought into custody, fingerprinted, and placed in a holding cell. It was the same one that Kirk and I waited in just before we were searched. I could see him with his head in his hands. I couldn't help but empathize with the man as he sat alone in that room. I had been where he now was.

It reminded me of when Ben Hur escaped as a slave on a galley ship, and was picked up by another ship. As he walked past the hold, he paused for a moment and listened to the dreadful noise of the condemned slaves as they pulled on the oars. It was a powerful moment, as he empathized with them. Yet, no doubt, he greatly appreciated the fact that he was free from those chains.

That's how I feel as I walk through this life. Empathy makes me feel the pain of those who still sit in the shadow of death. At the same time I am filled with a joy unspeakable that I am no longer chained to the law of sin and death. I violated an eternal Law, but my fine was paid and the prison door opened by the One who said, "I am He that lives, and was dead; and, behold, I am alive for evermore, Amen; and have the keys of hell and of death." Oh, what a Savior

"Whom having not seen, you love; in whom, though now you see him not, yet believing, you rejoice with joy unspeakable and full of glory" (1 Peter 1:8).

THE PLACE OF REPENTANCE

Someone wrote to me deeply concerned that I had said that repentance cannot save us. It can't. Moslems repent. That's the basis of their hope of salvation. It's the same with many Catholics who have never been born again. They trust that their repentance is enough. But no good judge would let a devious criminal go simply because he said that he had turned from his crimes.

The only thing that can save us is God's grace. Salvation is by grace through faith in Jesus. (See Ephesians 2:8-9.) The way to partake of the grace of God is through repentance, but repentance doesn't save us. If it did, we wouldn't need a Savior. Think of it like this. A man is in a rowboat that's about to go over Niagara Falls. Someone throws him a rope. He turns towards the rope, and then grabs it in faith. Will that save him? No. He turned. He took hold of the rope in faith. But if the person on the other end isn't pulling on the rope, he's still going over the falls.

God has thrown us a rope through the gospel. We turn in repentance and take hold of the Savior by faith. But it is the grace of God alone that saves us by drawing us to himself.

"For by grace are you saved through faith; and that not of yourselves: it is the gift of God: Not of works, lest any man should boast" (Ephesians 2:8-9).

A Strange Experience

I was reminded recently about a strange experience I had when I was preaching at a church. For some unknown reason during the sermon, the entire congregation called out the word, "Iniquity!" I thought I had suddenly committed some horrible sin, and was quite taken back by it. It was only later that I realized what had happened. I had said, "Jesus said, 'Depart  from me, you that work iniquity.' That word 'iniquity' means 'lawlessness.' The Book of Timothy says, 'Let everyone that names the name of Christ depart from 'iniquity.' Same word."

The congregation misunderstood my "Same word." They thought that I had said, "Say the word." So they did. Out loud.

"Wash me thoroughly from my iniquity, and cleanse me from my sin" (Psalm 51:2).

Tips for Witnessing and Open-air Preaching

Here are a couple of ways I have recently heard about to engage people when witnessing. Offer ten dollars to anyone who can name all ten of the Ten Commandments in order. Very few can. That will get groups of people quoting the Commandments and making it easy to ask who's kept what. Or, when open-air preaching and taking someone through the Good Person Test, appoint six people in the crowd to act as a jury. People are usually quick to judge other people's sins. That will help engage the crowd, and take the heat off you. Or when asking trivia questions, give Million Dollar Bill tracts away as consolation prizes to those who get the answer wrong, and Giant Money tracts to those who get them right. That way you can get tracts into more hands.

"... he that wins souls is wise" (Proverbs 11:30).

Heart-breaker

There's a website that's recently been in the news. It's called http://www.dogsindanger.com/ It shows pictures of cute and long-faced dogs who are soon to be put to death. It's controversial because they show a clock ticking the time down to when each dog will be put to sleep. That pulls on the heartstrings.

I would like to create a website called www.humansindanger.com with a clock ticking down to when human beings will be put to death. Every day 150,000 people die. The clock is ticking. Our hearts should more than break at the thought. We should be horrified that a single soul would end up in hell, and let that horror energize us, with God's help, to rescue them.

"For I have no pleasure in the death of him that dies, says the Lord God: therefore turn yourselves, and live" (Ezekiel 18:32).

Bizarre Experience

Three of us were walking on a sidewalk in San Antonio, Texas, on our way to a restaurant when a man joined us. He acted as though he was a best friend with Duane, our producer/director. Duane kept looking around at me as the guy talked to him, with an expression of "What's going on here?" When the three of us walked into the restaurant, the waiter asked, "How many?" and

we heard, "Four." It was the stranger that gave that number. He then sat down at our table and started yapping to us.

Then came a pitch for money. I told him he could have some if he would let me talk to him. I then went through the gospel and gave him five dollars. He then wanted me to pay for his meal as well, and kept on talking about being a workaholic. He had the "-holic" part right. Each of us could feel a spirit of anger in his voice. It was very intimidating. I told him that he was only getting the five dollars. I took hold of his hand, prayed for him, and he left. It was a bizarre experience.

"Strive to enter in at the strait gate: for many, I say to you, will seek to enter in, and shall not be able" (Luke 13:24).

How Much Cash

For those who think that giving money to church or to charities is a way to get to Heaven, the question becomes: how much qualifies me for entrance? To date, Bill Gates has given away $28,000,000,000 to charitable work. Is that enough? When is God impressed to a point where He is willing to sell immortality to a guilty sinner and be bribed to pervert eternal justice?

"But God said to him, You fool, this night your soul shall be required of you: then whose shall those things be, which you have provided? So is he that lays up treasure for himself, and is not rich toward God" (Luke 12:20-21).

"The Way of the Master"
Evidence Bible

Prove God's existence. Answer 100 common objections to Christianity. Show the Bible's supernatural origin. This unique study Bible includes wisdom from the foremost Christian leaders of yesterday and today such as Charles Spurgeon, D.L. Moody, John Wesley, Charles Finney, George Whitefield, Billy Graham, Dr. Bill Bright, John MacArthur, and R.C. Sproul.

Complete Bible available in
• Hardback
• Leather-bound (black or burgundy)
• Paperback

New Testament, Proverbs & Pslams available in
• Paperback
• Black leather-bound pocket editon

Bridge-Logos Titles from Ray Comfort to Help You Share Your Faith

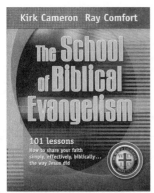

The School of Biblical Evangelism
In this comprehensive study course, you will learn how to share your faith simply, effectively, and biblically— the way Jesus did. Discover the God-given evangelistic tools that will enable you to confidently talk about the Savior.

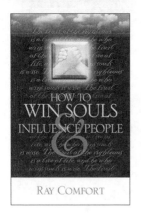

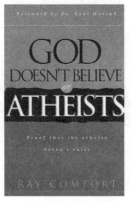

More **Bridge-Logos** Titles
from Ray Comfort

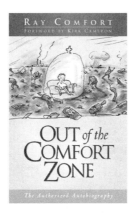

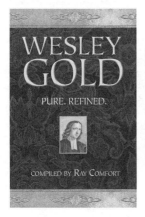

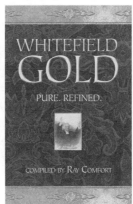

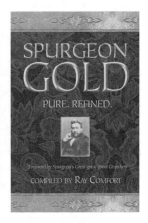